Outdoor Things to Do

Year-Round Nature Fun for Girls and Boys

BY WILLIAM HILLCOURT

ILLUSTRATED BY W. T. MARS

EDITORIAL DIRECTOR: ROBERT D. BEZUCHA

 Golden Press • New York

WESTERN PUBLISHING COMPANY, INC.
RACINE, WISCONSIN

CONTENTS

INTRODUCTION

Have you ever thought of yourself as a member of the crew of a spaceship whizzing through space?

Well, you are one! And you are traveling on a spaceship right this moment at the breakneck speed of more than 60,000 miles an hour as Spaceship Earth whirls through the universe!

On the spaceships that the United States sent into space, the crew members had names like John and Gordon, Edward and Walt, Neil and Edwin, among others. Each of these spacemen had specific duties to perform. All of them had to work closely together as a team. They were sustained by air and water and food. Their craft was speeded along by rocket fuel and guided by electricity.

On Spaceship Earth, the crew members are called People and Mammals, Birds and Fishes, Reptiles and Insects, Flowers and Trees, and by thousands of other names. Each of these crew members has a task to do. They, too, are sustained by the supplies on board—air and water and food. The energy for their living and guidance for their traveling are provided by the sun.

If a member of the crew of a man-made spaceship should fail in his duties or should pass out or even die in space, the lives of all the others would be in danger—the mission might end in disaster. This would also happen if the supplies should run out.

The same is the case with Spaceship Earth.

The duties and life of each crew member are completely tied in with the functions and lives of all the others. If even one crew member failed in the task assigned or died, all of Spaceship Earth would suffer. If several failed, life of all might fail, and a lifeless earth might be hustling through space.

It is only recently that we human beings have come to realize the importance of the relationships of all things in nature. If, for instance, certain plant life used for food should fail through drought, the immediate animal life would suffer, and human beings on the other side of the globe might starve. If certain birds should be killed off, a plague of the insects that formed their diet might denude the plant life of vast areas. If the waters of the oceans were polluted, all water life might die and turn the earth into a stink hole.

It is by truly understanding nature and by acting on this understanding that many future disasters can be averted. And the way to achieve this understanding is by studying nature on field trips and by undertaking activities and projects, each of them for a definite purpose.

And then, with understanding, will come an appreciation and love of nature that will result in a determination to safeguard all its living things and all its natural environments.

That's what *Outdoor Things to Do* is all about.

The nature trails in the Everglades National Park bring you into a unique and exciting environment.

HIT THE TRAIL!

"HIT THE TRAIL!" That's the big idea in all nature pursuits. To really learn about nature you must be out in nature—following the forest trails, hiking the hills, climbing the mountains, wading the streams, swimming the lakes. You must get close to the land—its soils, its rocks, its minerals. You must watch the birds in the sky and on their nests, the animals out in the open and in their hiding places. You must follow the seasons in the world of plants: notice the earliest sign of life in a flowering plant, see the flowers blooming, the seeds ripening; study a tree from the opening of its buds to the dropping of its fruits. You must lie under the stars and marvel at the wonders of the universe.

You must learn to make use of all your five senses: see the glory of the sunset, hear the call of the cardinal, smell the fragrance of the honeysuckle, taste the sweetness of the wild strawberry, feel the rain in your face.

So, get up and get out—"HIT THE TRAIL!" That's the beginning of all the "outdoor things to do" in this book. Every activity starts in the outdoors. It is only after an outdoor adventure that some things may still have to be done indoors—identifications to be checked, notes to be written, collections to be prepared.

Some of the outdoor things are done best if you do them alone—watching a bird nest from a blind, stalking an animal through the brush. Others are done best with a pal, for fun and for safety—skin diving for saltwater life, mountain climbing for studying a special rock formation. Still others are done best as family activities—finding shells at the seashore, attracting birds to your windows, caring for an aquarium, planting a wild-flower garden.

And then there are all the activities you can do with the gang—field trips to investigate certain environments, putting up a nature museum in classroom or patrol den, planting trees around the school grounds, making a nature trail in camp.

If you go it alone or with a pal, you can pretty well take off on your trail trips on the spur of the moment. With a group, you'll need to do a certain amount of advance planning to get the greatest value out of the trail expedition. If you can persuade a person knowledgeable on the subject you intend to pursue to come along, so much the better.

In the beginning, your trail expeditions may not take you too far away: you need to discover all the best trails within easy reach of your home. But soon you will want to get farther afield. Then comes the time when you take off to investigate the nearby parks of your state and, eventually, the national parks and wilderness areas of our country.

Today, nature trails have been established in practically every park. By following these trails through some of our national parks you will see natural wonders you won't find any other place on our globe.

In the Sequoia National Park in California, for instance, the trails take you in among the tallest and oldest trees in the world: the mighty sequoias, the tallest of them as tall as a 30-floor skyscraper and probably 3,000 years old. In the Everglades Park in Florida, you walk on boardwalks into this tremendous "river of grass"—7 million acres of it—to watch egrets and roseate spoonbills, wood storks and pelicans fly through the air, while alligators lurk in the waters below.

In the Grand Tetons in Wyoming, the animals you see along the trails may be elk and bighorn sheep, mule deer and moose, while the animals you encounter on the trails of the Shenandoah National Park, in Virginia, may be red and gray fox, white-tailed deer, bobcat and, perhaps, bear. And at Buck Island in the West Indies, you can snorkel along an underwater nature trail, swimming among brilliantly colored tropical fish.

The whole wide outdoors lies in front of you. By following the trails under the open sky and taking advantage of what they tell, you will not only get to learn some of the secrets of nature, you will also strengthen your body and improve your health, and, what is of great importance, you will have fun.

Put up brush shelters for wildlife.

Save victims of oil spills.

CLEANING STATION

Replant fire scars.

Clean junk from roadside.

OUR NATURAL RESOURCES

The more field trips you take, the more you will come to appreciate the beauty of nature. The more, also, you will come to realize that "nature" is not just one thing—"nature" is a multitude of things with tremendous variety.

The nature of a forest is vastly different from the nature of a desert or a meadow or a seashore. The nature you find at the top of a mountain is completely different from what you find at the foot. Each of these nature areas is its own kind of environment: a home for particular animals and plants that live together, depending for their survival on each other and on the conditions that surround them, of sunlight and shade, temperature and humidity, moisture in the ground or in the air, good soil or poor soil, and many other things. Each environment is a complex system, an ecosystem—a word based on Greek *oikos,* meaning home. The study of environments, of the relationship between living things and their surroundings, is called ecology.

Undisturbed, nature's ecosystems can go on for thousands of years. That was the case of America's virgin forests and prairies, lakes and rivers—until the white man arrived and began upsetting the systems by clearing the forests for towns and cities, breaking the prairie for farmland, developing the waterways for transportation.

And so, on your hikes, you will not only see the beauty of nature. You will also notice the scars of civilization—not just the big scars, deliberately planned, of roads and highways, bridges and viaducts, mines and quarries, but also scars caused by accident or carelessness —beaches blackened by oil spills, forests destroyed by fires, rivers polluted by industrial wastes. And more and more today, scars caused by thoughtlessness or deliberate vandalism—smashed bottles on a bathing beach, old tires and other debris in a river, beer cans and plastic cups and soggy cardboard boxes and other junk along the roadside.

Over recent years, the American public has begun to wake up to the fact that wilderness areas once destroyed may never flourish again, that rivers and lakes once polluted may never clear themselves, that mineral resources used wastefully are gone forever, that certain wildlife is in danger of extinction. More and more, people are joining together in environmental societies or ecological groups to work for the conservation of our natural resources. Youth groups, such as Boy Scouts and Girl Scouts, Camp Fire Girls and 4-H Clubs, are vigorously engaged in conservation activities.

As you go about your nature pursuits, what can you do as a single individual?

Funny part is that you'll have to start by deciding on things you will NOT do. You need to become conservation-minded and decide that you will *not* put a scar on the landscape by dropping your trash along the trail, you will *not* damage trees, you will *not* wantonly pick rare plants and flowers, you will *not* cut across cultivated fields, you will *not* build a picnic fire on a spot from which the fire may spread.

When it comes to doing things, you will accomplish most by working with others in the cause of conservation.

Join some group of like-minded people interested in ecology and environmental protection; take part in the group's discussions and its deliberations and its various projects. Make yourself available in community efforts for cleaning up a local park or river or roadside. Volunteer your services when some special damage needs to be overcome.

In all such work, come properly prepared with suitable clothing and whatever tools and special equipment may be required.

When cleaning up a stream, for instance, protect your feet with sneakers or other tough footwear, your legs with coarse jeans, your hands with work gloves. For cleaning up a roadside area, use work clothes and work gloves and have rakes and garbage cans on hand. For working in an oil spill, use old clothes and gloves that can be thrown away. For planting trees, you'll require tools for digging holes; for building brush shelters for the winter protection of small animals, you may want axes for cutting deadwood.

In case of a clean-up job you will also need to arrange transportation for bringing the debris to the local dump for disposal. In most cases, the sanitation department of your community will be willing to come to your assistance.

So go to it! America needs your help.

Join an existing conservation club or form one of your own, with some of your friends.

When cleaning a stream of rubbish, protect your feet, legs, and hands against cuts.

Put out a small fire correctly: Sprinkle— do not pour—water on embers. Stir with a stick. When wetted down, feel with palm of hand.

NATURE GARDENS AND MUSEUMS

If you happen to be a city boy or girl, you may only be able to strike out on wilderness trails on special occasions—on holidays or vacations. This does not mean that you can't learn about nature in a big way during in-between times. On the contrary. Practically every large city has some outdoor areas—botanical and zoological gardens—specifically dedicated to the study and enjoyment of nature, and indoor natural history museums. Even if you live in a smaller community, you may find in it a local or state, or college or university museum. Your own school may have a limited museum specializing in the natural history of your immediate vicinity.

In a botanical garden you have a chance to follow the growth of trees and flowering plants throughout the seasons. In such a garden you would not just be walking among pines and firs, or oaks and beeches, or maples and hickories, as you would in a natural forest. Trees would have been brought in to represent all the different forest types in your state, perhaps in the whole country. In addition to trees you would also have an opportunity to learn about other plants. Most botanical gardens have large areas set aside for local wild flowers. A garden in a northern state might even contain a hothouse with semitropical plants that flourish in spite of the howling winter storm outside.

In modern zoological gardens, every effort is made to make the environment of each animal resemble as closely as possible the environment in which it usually lives. So you may see mountain goats jumping among crags that look like those they climb in nature, beavers building a hut in a large pool, prairie dogs scurrying into their burrows, porcupines taking life easy in a rest tree.

Most of these zoological gardens have a special section for snakes and turtles—called a herpetarium—and another for birds—called an aviary. Generally, an aviary consists of a number of large cages with birds for you to watch from the outside. But the modern way is to construct a large cage that you can enter to find yourself among walking birds, with other birds flying over your head.

The zoological garden might also have a special section with large tanks full of native and exotic fish, although, in many cities, such a display is contained in a separate aquarium. Here you can get to know our native fish so that you will be able to recognize your catch next time you go fishing.

For an even more concentrated education in nature, you can't beat a well-organized natural history museum.

Many of these museums, today, have large diorama landscapes showing complete ecosystems: natural environments with their specific plant and animal life and geological features. Here the animals and birds, reptiles and fishes, are not alive but are stuffed specimens that represent the very finest examples of a taxidermist's skills. Nor are the trees and plants alive and growing—the leaves and flowers are skillfully made from plastic and skillfully put together to look like the real things.

The special value of such an exhibit is that everything stays put, giving you a chance for thorough observation and finding everything there is to find. In addition, each such exhibit will have signs that tell you about what you see, providing you with names and special information.

In addition to these natural-looking exhibits, the natural history museums also have educational displays where animals and plants, rocks and minerals, are arranged in their scientific relationships—by their orders and families.

In all these exhibits, pay special attention to those that show and explain local or regional plant and animal life and geology. By observing carefully and by reading the signs and remembering what you have seen and read, you are well on your way to recognizing the same animals and plants, rocks and minerals, when you come upon them in their natural surroundings.

In a planetarium, special complex projectors show the movement of stars and planets on a large dome.

In a mineralogical museum, minerals and rocks are arranged according to scientific classifications.

After studying the exhibits of a good museum, you'll have an idea of how to develop your own.

NATURE SKETCHING

Buy a sketch pad and a soft pencil, then go to work. Use a light touch in outlining your subject. Next fill in the details.

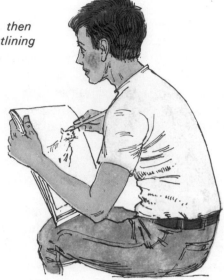

Begin your nature sketching by drawing your pet dog or cat in various positions.

In nature, a bird begins as an egg. So does a sketch of a bird.

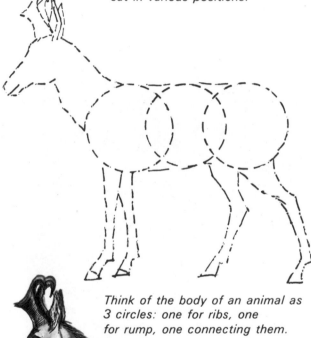

Think of the body of an animal as 3 circles: one for ribs, one for rump, one connecting them.

The bodies of some birds are chunky egg-shaped, others are elongated.

Sketch in the animal's head next, then the legs.

Toes and nails may prove the hardest part.

NATURE SKETCHING

Even if you have only the slightest amount of drawing ability, you can get a lot of enjoyment out of nature sketching.

The equipment is simple: just a sketch pad and a soft pencil or, if you prefer, a charcoal stick or crayons. Also, probably, an eraser.

Get accustomed from the start to drawing rapidly, with determined strokes. Get the outline of your subject down quickly, then fill in the details. To make your sketches more permanent, you may want to go over the lines with pen and ink or with a felt pen after you get home from your nature hike.

If you are interested in animals and have a dog or cat of your own, start by sketching your pet. Begin with a straight side view, then catch your pet in other positions—feeding, playing, jumping, sleeping.

For other nature subjects it may be smart of you first to copy from different nature books.

But the real fun comes when you take sketch pad and pencil with you on a nature hike and bring home a whole slew of sketches you have made in your own inimitable style.

Sketch fish in front of an aquarium: 2 arcs for the body, then fins, tail, head.

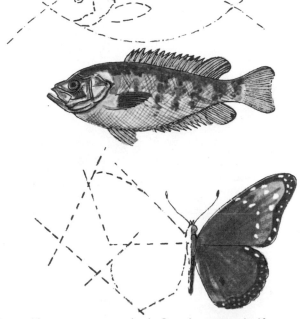

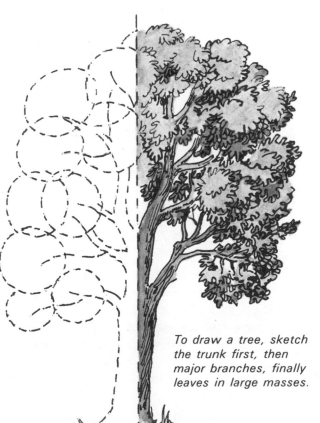

To draw a tree, sketch the trunk first, then major branches, finally leaves in large masses.

Butterflies are symmetrical. So, draw one half of the insect, then the other half to match.

 For most flowers, begin with oval or circular outline.

Leaves, like butterflies, are symmetrical. Draw one half, then the other half. Finish with the veins.

BLACK AND WHITE

There is special enjoyment to developing your own films in your own darkroom.

In doing your own enlarging, you can compose your pictures for greatest effect.

COLOR

Color slides have wide use for study and entertainment.

Color prints are spectacular— and expensive.

Color movies are the ultimate in nature photography.

NATURE PHOTOGRAPHY

Most likely you already have a camera and have been shooting friends and relatives for years. Whatever camera you own can be used for general nature photography and probably also for taking certain specialized pictures. The first step, then, is for you to really learn what your camera can do. So get out again the instruction book that came with the camera and study it carefully.

Even if yours is a low-priced, fixed-focus camera you may find that by slipping inexpensive close-up lenses over the regular lens, you can get close enough to almost any nature subject to take an interesting picture.

Later on, if nature photography becomes a real hobby for you, you may want to get a better camera with a couple of extra lenses suitable for advanced photography.

In that case you will almost certainly shift to a single-reflex camera which, today, is the most popular camera for all types of nature photography.

Your best bet, in the beginning, is to go in for *black and white photography.* The exact exposure is not as critical in black and white as it is in photographing in color, and you have a chance to experiment with your negatives, particularly if you can manage to set up a small darkroom of your own. Such a darkroom makes it possible for you to do your own film developing and to produce your own prints. In making your enlargements you are able to blow up whatever parts of your negatives will make the most spectacular pictures. In this way, a nature subject—a flower or a bird, for instance—that only takes up a small part of the negative may be enlarged to fill a whole sheet of photographic paper.

Most amateur *color photography* consists of making color slides that can be projected onto a screen for your own satisfaction or for showing other people the wonders of nature. Any camera that takes 35mm films can be used for making color slides. In taking color shots it is very important to get the exposure just right. To assure the correct exposure you will need a good exposure meter—unless the camera you have has a built-in meter of its own.

The lens plays an important part in the picture you get. The standard lens is suitable for general nature photography.

For semi-close-ups you must either have a lens of a greater focal length or be able to get nearer to your subject.

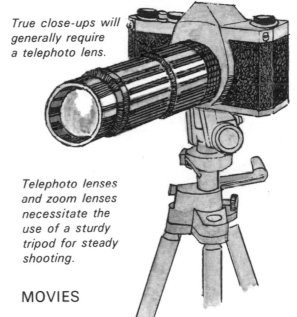

True close-ups will generally require a telephoto lens.

Telephoto lenses and zoom lenses necessitate the use of a sturdy tripod for steady shooting.

MOVIES

Some day you may decide to take the step from making still pictures of nature into the much more complicated field of producing nature movies. Here you will need special equipment and special films—but even more important, you will need infinite patience for getting your footage and great discrimination in cutting it down and editing it into a film that your audience will be interested in seeing.

Most nature photography requires a sturdy tripod. Best for movies is an elevator tripod with pan head.

Photos of mammals will mainly be night shots. Get the right kind of flashgun to fit your camera.

With an extra-long cable release you can snap shutter from a distance of 12'.

Set up camera where animal feeds. Snap when it sits still.

Use long cable or tube release to snap bird on perch.

In a mirror fastened to camera you can watch bird or butterfly for best pose.

TRICKS IN NATURE PHOTOGRAPHY

For nature photography you can't get along without a tripod. This is particularly true if you use a telephoto lens: the weight of the lens makes the camera front-heavy and almost impossible to hold in your hand. A regular, sturdy tripod will do for all still photography, but in making movies you need a tripod with a "pan head" that will make it possible for you to take panorama shots, whether horizontally of a landscape or vertically of a tree trunk, or to follow the soaring of gulls or the flight of a deer.

Since many animals move about only by twilight or in the depth of night you will need a good flashgun if you expect to photograph them. Get the type that is recommended for your camera and learn everything it will do by studying the instruction book carefully. For twilight photography, you can set up a feeding area, baiting it with the kind of food the animal likes. Put up the camera, with flashgun in place, in a suitable location, and remove yourself, ready to snap the shutter, as far as the wire of a long cable release (up to 12 feet) or the tube of an air bulb release (30 feet or more) will permit. For dark night photography, you can set up your camera along the animal's runway, with a trip line attached to the camera release and arranged in such a way that the animal can take its own photograph. The gadget that does the trick may be made of a couple of pieces of wood, hinged together and snapped together by the force of a couple of rubber bands when a thin trigger stick between them is removed or broken. In all probability you will be able to invent for yourself the kind of remote release that will best fit your camera.

You will also need to come up with a trick way of photographing if you want to take shots of the fish in your aquarium. Here, also, artificial light is necessary. A flash can't be used—

For aquarium photography, make box for camera. Light tank from top and sides.

Glass pane keeps fish in focus.

Construct remote release from wood pieces. Attach trip cord to thin notched stick.

adjustable screw

rubber band

notch

rubber band

notch

cable release

it will only be reflected into your camera from the front glass of the aquarium. Regular shooting with a floodlight is out—you will mainly get the reflection of your camera in the glass. So, for successful aquarium photography, you get a cardboard box that fits the front of the tank, cut a hole in it to accommodate your camera lens, and set it up in front of the tank. To keep the fish in focus, you imprison them between the front of the tank and a pane of glass, placed inside the tank a couple of inches from the front. By lighting the tank properly, with floodlights at the sides and above, you should be able to get just the shots you want. But turn the lights off between shots so that you do not heat up the water unnecessarily.

Remote release may also be made with a corner iron. (See illustration above.)

White-breasted Nuthatch

Belted Kingfisher

Redheaded Woodpecker

Black-capped Chickadee

Cardinal

Great Horned Owl

Bald Eagle

House Wren

Common Snipe

Blue Jay

Ruby-throated Hummingbird

Yellow-shafted Flicker

Yellow-billed Cuckoo

Great Blue Heron

Crow

Virginia Rail

American Avocet

Canada Goose

Sage Grouse

American Woodcock

Wood Duck

Common Loon

Whistling Swan

18

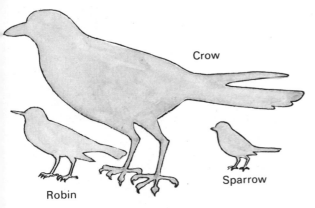

Crow

Robin

Sparrow

BIRDS

Many people take birds for granted. To them birds are simply animals that have feathers and fly through the air. They give no special thought to the astonishing feat that flying is.

For thousands of years, man dreamed of being able to fly. Everything worked against him. He might make himself artificial wings in imitation of bird wings—but his body was too heavy, his strength too weak. He finally got off the ground, but only thanks to powerful engines.

Birds are created for flight. Their bodies are streamlined and extraordinarily light for their size because their bones are hollow and air sacs are distributed throughout their bodies like tiny balloons. Their arms have become wings, with feathers in overlapping patterns that assure the greatest possible resistance to the air on the downward stroke, the least possible on the upbeat. And the breast muscles that move the wings have been developed to astonishing strength.

So, begin your study of birds by an appreciation of that flying ability that varies with each species—from short, quick flight to soaring.

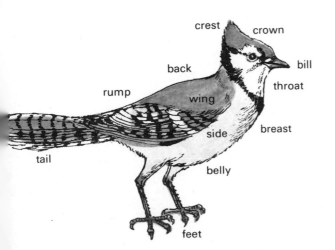

crest crown
back bill
throat
rump
wing
side breast
tail
belly
feet

You'll have a much better time on your bird hikes if you can recognize the birds you see, and know them by their names. In the beginning, the best way to learn is to go hiking with someone who knows about birds. But soon you will be able to identify the birds on your own with the help of a good bird book that indicates all the identifying points, along the following lines:

SIZE You can easily see the importance of noticing the size when you realize that you may come upon birds as tiny as hummingbirds and as large as great blue herons. So learn to estimate the size as compared with some familiar bird: ''about the size of a song sparrow'' (6''), ''slightly smaller than a robin'' (10''), or ''almost as big as a crow'' (19'').

SHAPE Some birds are long and slim, others short and plump. Some, such as ducks, have short legs; others, like herons, have them long. The tail may be short like a meadowlark's, long like a mockingbird's, or in-between like a robin's. It may be pointed or squared or forked. The bill may be slender or sharp, or broad and conical. The head may be rounded or crested.

COLORS The general color will sometimes identify your bird: the black of a crow, the bright red of the scarlet tanager, the blue of the indigo bunting. But many birds can be told apart only by their special markings: by spots or streaks on their breasts, bands on their tails, bars on their wings, stripes over their eyes or on their crowns.

FLIGHT How does the bird fly? In a straight line, or dipping up and down, or in a zigzag pattern? Does it fly with slow or fast wingbeats? There's no mistaking a swallow's skimming flight over a lake, the soaring of an eagle, the bounding of a woodpecker.

SONG Very often the first you will know of a bird's presence is its song or call. You will soon get to know the cowbird, squeaking like a rusty hinge, the blue jay screaming its call, the chickadee saying its name. You will get to know the redwing by its gurgling song, the hermit thrush by its flutelike melody, the meadowlark by its clear musical whistle.

SURROUNDINGS Some birds prefer open fields, others woods, still others marshland or lakes. Small birds haunting the shores of ponds, streams, oceans are pretty certain to be sandpipers, snipes, plovers. Small brownish birds in the fields are almost as certainly members of the sparrow tribe.

BIRD WALKING

Among people, young and old, who love nature, bird walking is probably their most popular activity. It combines the healthy physical sport of hiking with the mental exercises of observing and remembering. When once your interest in birds has been caught you will have a hobby that will last for the rest of your life.

In the beginning, you will probably not go very far afield in your bird walking, but will concentrate on the birds right around your own neighborhood. They will give you many hours of enjoyment when once you start watching them. But it won't be long before you will want to go bird hiking in fields and forests, along the edges of marshes and swamps, along lakeshores and seashores, perhaps into the desert and up into the mountains.

You will then find that each kind of environment will have its own kind of bird life. And you will also discover that in our vast America, with its varying climates and landscape features, many of the birds you see in the northern states will be different from those you see in the South, and those in the West different from the birds of the East.

The best time for bird walking is early morning, from daybreak to about two hours

Every environment in our vast America has its own special kind of bird life.

Use field glasses for scanning area for birds.

later. That's the time of day when birds are particularly active. Dress warmly—mornings are often cool. Bring along notebook and pencil, bird guide, and field glasses.

When you get into bird territory, move quietly, without any vigorous motions, and keep your eyes and ears wide open. So far as possible, stalk with the sun at your back. The sun will then shine full on the birds in front of you. When the sun is in your face, all birds will appear as dark silhouettes.

When you see a bird, stop and watch it carefully. Notice its size and its field marks so that you will be able to identify it in your bird guide if you don't already know it.

At certain times of year be prepared for sudden showers.

Dress warmly for early morning bird walking— especially in spring and fall.

Bring along a snack and a hot drink for mid-morning break.

Field glasses are indispensable for studying birds.

Always carry your bird guide with you.

21

A step ladder makes an easy blind. Provide it with a seat. Cover it with green or camouflaged cloth, with net window for observation, and zipper door.

For seashore observation, a low, triangular tent is suitable. Pitch it with 3 poles, or 2 poles and a rope ridge. Provide it with window and door.

GETTING CLOSE TO BIRDS

Watching birds through binoculars from a distance is not always satisfactory—particularly not when you have discovered a bird on the nest. You want to get near to see what goes on. You can do that by putting up a blind close to the nest.

A blind is simply a hiding place from which to watch a bird without disturbing it by your presence. The designs on this page will give you an idea about the kind you may want.

Persuade an electrician to do the bending with his wall conduit bender.

Wall conduits fit snugly into holes in wooden block.

A lightweight, collapsible bird blind can be made from 6 lengths of ½'' electrical wall conduit, bent and inserted into a circular wooden block.

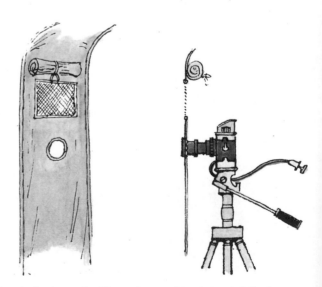

A window made of netting makes it possible for you to see the bird without the bird seeing you. Cut a circular hole to fit lens of your camera.

To attract birds to a garden, put in berry-bearing bushes for fruit-eating birds; large seed-bearing annuals for birds that prefer a diet of seeds.

Well-stocked feeding trays and well-built bird houses will bring birds into your garden. So will a shallow bird bath kept filled with clear water.

GETTING BIRDS CLOSE TO YOU

Instead of trying to get yourself close to the birds you want to watch, you may like to have the birds come close to you.

Out in the field you can do this by imitating their calls and their songs.

All bird watchers go in for "squeaking." This is a sound you make with your lips against the back of your hand. It resembles the scream given off by a bird in distress. Almost immediately, some curious birds will fly near to find out what's up.

To attract specific birds, you need to learn to reproduce their specific songs or calls: the clear whistles of robins and chickadees and many others, the mournful calls of doves and cuckoos, the harsh cries of jays and crows, the hoot of owls.

Close to home, if you have a garden you can attract birds to it all year round—in the winter by putting up feeding trays and keeping them supplied with food, in the spring by providing birdhouses, in the summer by growing berry-bearing bushes, such as raspberries and blackberries, and in the fall by seeing to it that sunflower, kafir corn, and millet seeds, sown early in the year, have a chance to ripen.

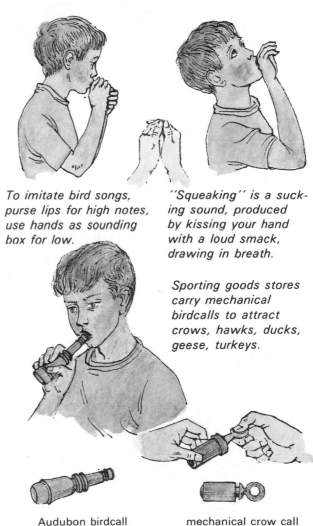

To imitate bird songs, purse lips for high notes, use hands as sounding box for low.

"Squeaking" is a sucking sound, produced by kissing your hand with a loud smack, drawing in breath.

Sporting goods stores carry mechanical birdcalls to attract crows, hawks, ducks, geese, turkeys.

Audubon birdcall   mechanical crow call

Red-eyed Vireo

Blue Jay

Flicker

Robin

Baltimore Oriole

Catbird

Snipe

House Wren

BIRD NEST COLLECTION

Keep the ground nest of a field sparrow in a cardboard box.

Use a block of wood as foundation for crotch with catbird nest.

Fasten branch with oriole nest to board and hang as a wall decoration.

Spray nests with insecticide to kill off mites and insects.

BIRD NESTS

There are two good times for finding bird nests. The first is in the spring. At that time the birds are busily occupied building their nests and feeding their young, and give away the locations of their nests by their flights back and forth. The other time is in the fall when the trees are bare and the nests are exposed to view.

Each bird has its own way of building a nest and its own preference for its location.

Some birds are satisfied with very primitive nests placed directly on the ground: killdeer in an open field, woodcock in the woods, Wilson's snipe in a marsh, common tern on the beach. Other birds build better-constructed nests of grass or twigs: redwing attaching its nest to cattails or reeds, catbird using the crotch of a bush, bluebird the hollow of a tree trunk. Still other birds go in for more elaborate architecture: Baltimore oriole suspending its nest from a branch high up in an elm, red-eyed vireo hanging its basketlike nest in the fork of a branch, robin making a cup-shaped nest from mud.

Once you have located a bird nest, there are several kinds of bird collecting you can undertake: the feathers you find on the ground below it, the pellets under the nest of an owl, the nest itself after the young have left. A nest display can be very attractive, especially if it contains a clutch of "eggs" made from plaster of paris and painted to look like the real thing.

BIRD FEATHERS

When bird hiking, bring along an envelope. When you find a feather, put it in the envelope for protection. Eventually, mount the feathers on sheets of cardboard.

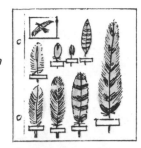

A loose-leaf binder is good for a feather collection.

OWL PELLETS

A collection of owl pellets might consist of whole pellets and the parts of a pellet glued to cardboard.

BIRD "EGGS"

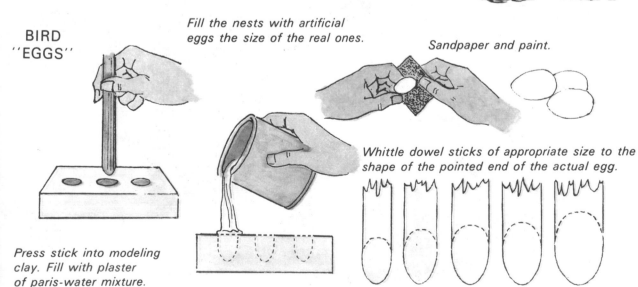

Fill the nests with artificial eggs the size of the real ones.

Sandpaper and paint.

Press stick into modeling clay. Fill with plaster of paris-water mixture.

Whittle dowel sticks of appropriate size to the shape of the pointed end of the actual egg.

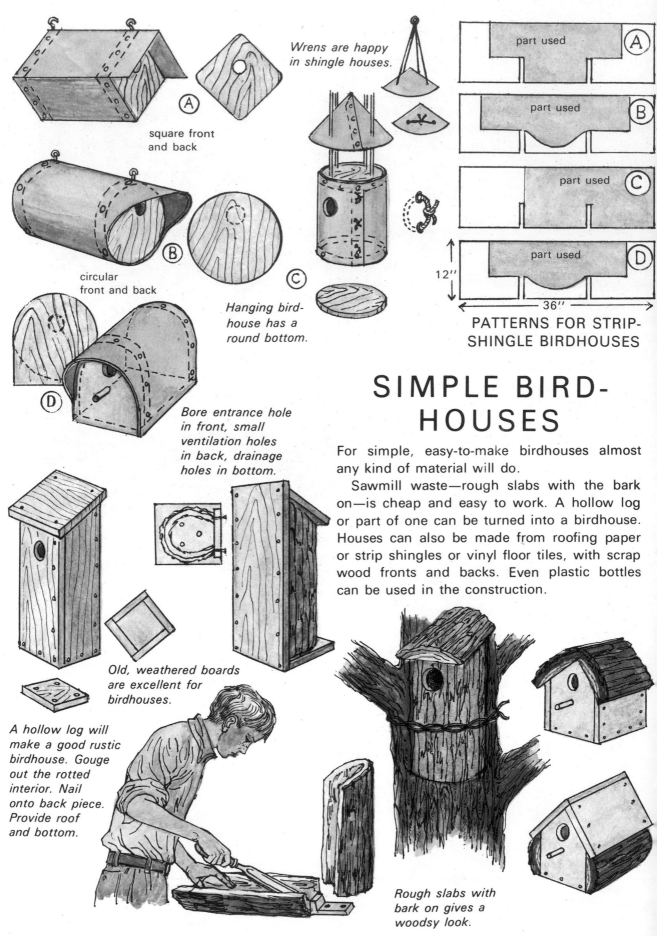

square front
and back

circular
front and back

Wrens are happy
in shingle houses.

Hanging bird-
house has a
round bottom.

Bore entrance hole
in front, small
ventilation holes
in back, drainage
holes in bottom.

12''

36''

PATTERNS FOR STRIP-
SHINGLE BIRDHOUSES

part used Ⓐ

part used Ⓑ

part used Ⓒ

part used Ⓓ

SIMPLE BIRD-HOUSES

For simple, easy-to-make birdhouses almost any kind of material will do.

Sawmill waste—rough slabs with the bark on—is cheap and easy to work. A hollow log or part of one can be turned into a birdhouse. Houses can also be made from roofing paper or strip shingles or vinyl floor tiles, with scrap wood fronts and backs. Even plastic bottles can be used in the construction.

Old, weathered boards
are excellent for
birdhouses.

A hollow log will
make a good rustic
birdhouse. Gouge
out the rotted
interior. Nail
onto back piece.
Provide roof
and bottom.

Rough slabs with
bark on gives a
woodsy look.

26

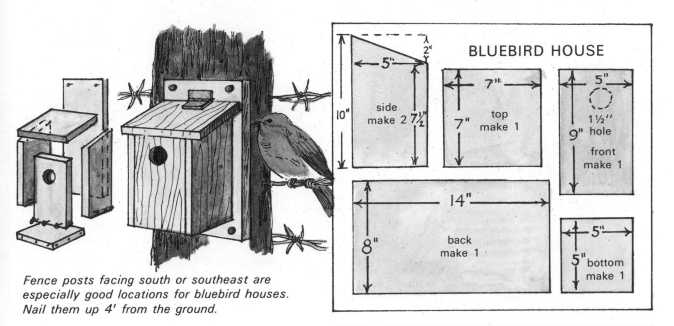

Fence posts facing south or southeast are especially good locations for bluebird houses. Nail them up 4' from the ground.

PLANS FOR BIRDHOUSES

There is an effective way of getting to know a few birds intimately. And that is by encouraging them to take up residence close to your home, by providing them with housing for their nests.

In making such houses, three points are of importance: proper size for the bird you want to attract, proper diameter of the entrance hole, proper height above the ground.

Wrens and chickadees, for instance, like houses with 4'' by 4'' bottoms, about 7'' high, with the entrance hole 1'' in diameter and 6'' above the floor. The houses should be placed 6 to 8 feet above the ground.

Certain swallows, flycatchers and finches go for houses slightly larger: 6'' by 6'' bottoms, 10'' high, with the entrance hole 1¼'' in diameter and 7'' above the floor. These houses should be placed up about 12 feet.

Robins and phoebes prefer pulpit-shaped brackets rather than boxes, about 7'' by 8'' by 9'', with at least one side open, placed 10 feet above the ground.

All houses should be well ventilated by slits or holes under the eaves. They can be easily drained of rain by ¼'' holes drilled in the bottom.

For better-quality birdhouses, use soft lumber about ½'' thick—pine, fir, cypress, redwood. Stain the outside, or paint the birdhouse in a dull, woodsy color—green or brown.

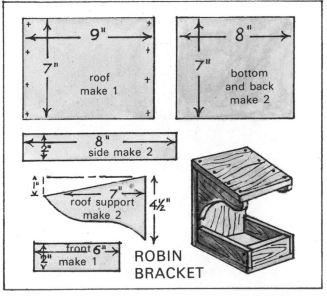

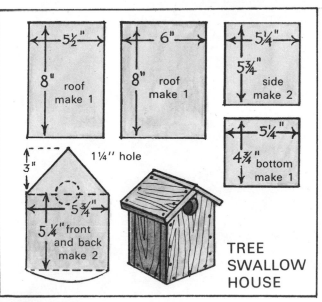

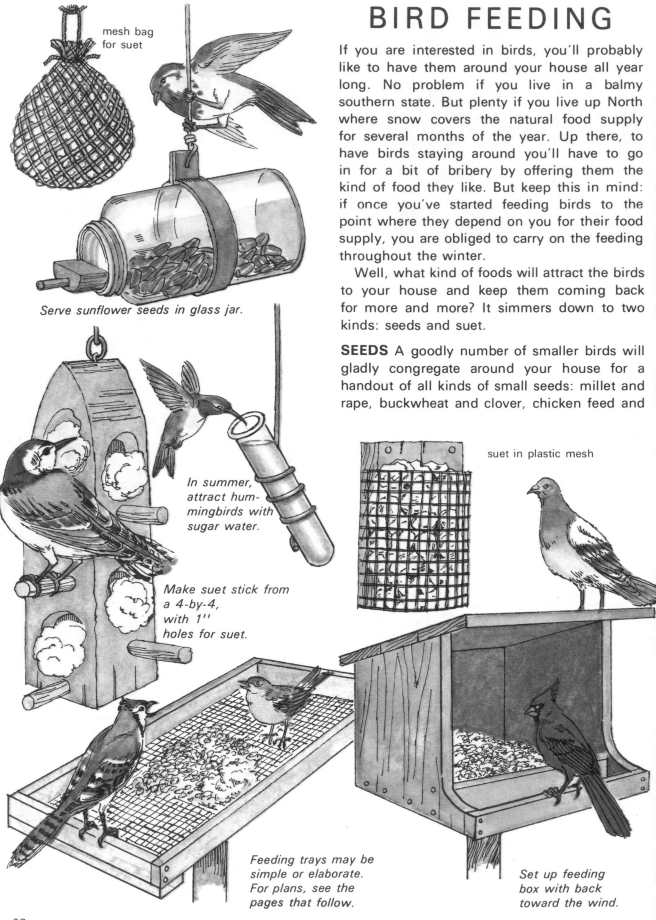

BIRD FEEDING

If you are interested in birds, you'll probably like to have them around your house all year long. No problem if you live in a balmy southern state. But plenty if you live up North where snow covers the natural food supply for several months of the year. Up there, to have birds staying around you'll have to go in for a bit of bribery by offering them the kind of food they like. But keep this in mind: if once you've started feeding birds to the point where they depend on you for their food supply, you are obliged to carry on the feeding throughout the winter.

Well, what kind of foods will attract the birds to your house and keep them coming back for more and more? It simmers down to two kinds: seeds and suet.

SEEDS A goodly number of smaller birds will gladly congregate around your house for a handout of all kinds of small seeds: millet and rape, buckwheat and clover, chicken feed and

mesh bag for suet

Serve sunflower seeds in glass jar.

In summer, attract hummingbirds with sugar water.

Make suet stick from a 4-by-4, with 1'' holes for suet.

suet in plastic mesh

Feeding trays may be simple or elaborate. For plans, see the pages that follow.

Set up feeding box with back toward the wind.

the "wildbird seed" mixture sold in many supermarkets. These seeds can be served on protected feeding trays and in special bird feeders (see next pages). They may bring in juncos and finches, tree sparrows and song sparrows, grosbeaks and buntings, perhaps a cardinal or two—and, of course, house sparrows.

Larger seeds, such as sunflower seeds, soybeans, whole and cracked corn, shelled peanuts, kafir corn, sorghum, wheat, and rye, may attract a number of larger birds: pheasants and grouse, quail and mourning doves. Broadcast the seed on the ground or on top of the snow, in a sheltered spot.

Seed-eating birds will also gladly accept a meal of bread and cracker crumbs, bits of doughnut and cake, cornflakes, stale cookies.

SUET Beef suet, firm, white or yellowish, comes in large lumps and is favored by birds that usually keep to a diet of worms and grubs, caterpillars and full-grown insects. That goes for chickadees and tufted titmice, downy and hairy and other woodpeckers, nuthatches and creepers, and, of course, blue jays, starlings, and grackles.

Suet can be served in many fashions. The simplest is merely tying it onto tree branches. Suet may also be hung in a mesh bag or put in a container of plastic mesh.

A more spectacular way of serving suet is by means of a suet stick. This is a length of a log or 4-by-4 into which has been bored a number of holes, 1" in diameter. Press suet firmly into each hole, screw a screw eye into one end of the log, and hang it high up in a tree. Should it be provided with perches? That's up to you. Most of the birds mentioned above will get along beautifully without perches. But house sparrows, starlings, and jays will have a hard time finding a foothold on a smooth, perchless suet stick.

If you can't manage to get suet, invent some kind of fatty substitute. A cheap peanut butter will do if stirred up with cornmeal to make it stiffer. So will a mixture of lard and bread crumbs.

The ultimate in serving suet is to use it for turning your discarded Christmas tree into a "bird tree." For this, set up the tree outdoors, in full view of your windows, then render the fat out of the suet and pour it onto the branches. Add any decorations that suit your fancy.

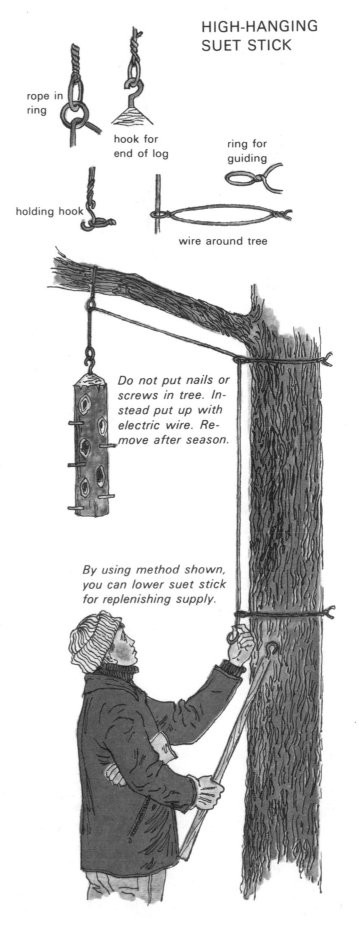

HIGH-HANGING SUET STICK

rope in ring

hook for end of log

ring for guiding

holding hook

wire around tree

Do not put nails or screws in tree. Instead put up with electric wire. Remove after season.

By using method shown, you can lower suet stick for replenishing supply.

SETTING UP BIRD-HOUSES AND FEEDERS

After you have made your birdhouses or bird feeders, the next step is to set them up.

Generally speaking, a birdhouse should be placed in open shade, on a pole or attached to a tree trunk, preferably with the entrance facing east or south.

A simple, tray-shaped bird feeder can be placed on brackets right outside your window. A more elaborate feeder may be put on a post close enough to the house for you to watch the visitors from a window.

To keep cats away from birdhouse, make a metal shield from tin cans with top and bottom removed and with side cut along the seam. Or make shield from sheet of aluminum.

Post may be set up between 2 U beams. By using 2 loosely inserted nails, lower nail may be removed for tipping house down for cleaning (see procedure, bottom of page). House or feeder may be attached to square post with help of brackets.

You can use galvanized pipe for setting up houses and feeders. Screw 1'' flange onto wooden bottom. Set suitable length of 1¼'' pipe in ground. Screw length of 1'' pipe into flange. Place the thinner pipe in pipe in ground. Set at proper height with nail (see details right and left).

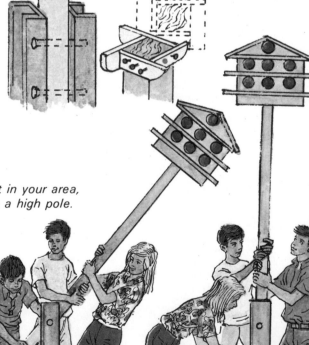

Purple martins live in colonies. If martins are abundant in your area, build an ''apartment house'' for them and put it up on a high pole.

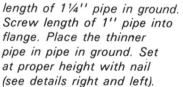

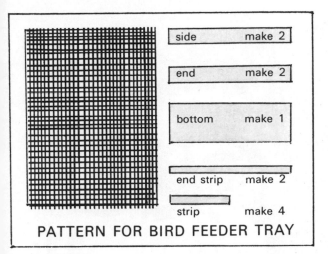

PATTERN FOR BIRD FEEDER TRAY

side	make 2
end	make 2
bottom	make 1
end strip	make 2
strip	make 4

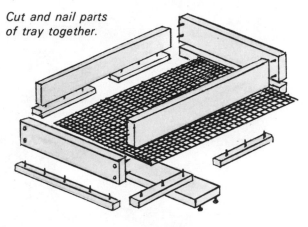

Cut and nail parts of tray together.

Tray feeder has 2'' sides to keep the food from being blown off.

BIRD FEEDERS

The kind of bird feeder you will want to put up will depend on where you live.

If you are an apartment dweller, your feeder will amount to a tray outside the window. This can be made from a board or a piece of plywood, with thin wood strips along the sides and front to keep the feed from blowing off.

A bird feeder in the country can be made as elaborate as you want it. The best model is along the line of a topless box lying on one side. Such a feeder may be suspended in such a way that it will turn and thereby always face away from whatever winter wind is blowing.

A box feeder is fundamentally an open box set up with its opening facing away from the wind. It can have a slanting or a straight roof as you prefer.

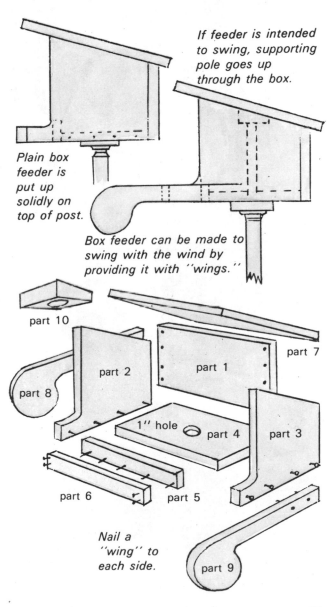

If feeder is intended to swing, supporting pole goes up through the box.

Plain box feeder is put up solidly on top of post.

Box feeder can be made to swing with the wind by providing it with "wings."

part 10

part 7

part 2

part 1

part 8

1'' hole   part 4

part 3

part 6   part 5

Nail a "wing" to each side.

part 9

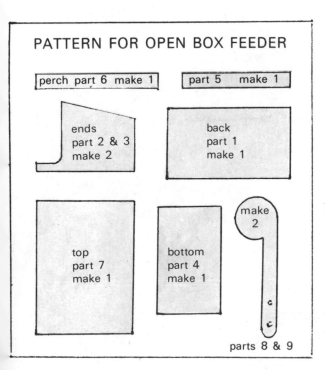

PATTERN FOR OPEN BOX FEEDER

| perch part 6 make 1 | part 5   make 1 |

ends
part 2 & 3
make 2

back
part 1
make 1

top
part 7
make 1

bottom
part 4
make 1

make 2

parts 8 & 9

Bat

Brown Bear

Badger

Muskrat

Shrew

Skunk

Opossum

Antelope

Porcupine

Fox

Elk

Rabbit

Woodchuck

Raccoon

Field Mouse

Squirrel

Moose

Beaver

OUR NORTH AMERICAN MAMMALS

The mammals are the furry, four-legged, warm-blooded creatures that roam the woods and the fields, the prairies and deserts of our country. They are called mammals because the very young are fed by the milk from their mothers' breasts, scientifically known as ''mammae.''

If you want to study mammals, your best procedure is to find out first what kinds live in your locality. Read up about them to learn about their habits. In this way, you will get to know where and when to find them.

It's mostly a matter of keeping your eyes wide open. Wherever you go, watch out for tracks and runways and feeding signs. In open fields, look for burrows that may shelter woodchucks or gophers or other burrowing animals. In marshy areas, keep an eye out for the houses of muskrats and beavers. Along a lake shore, locate the spots where animals come down to drink. And when you come upon a hollow tree, study it from top to bottom: you may discover the nest of a gray or flying squirrel in a small cavity in a high-up branch, of a raccoon or opossum in a larger hole in the trunk, and possibly the lair of a fox at the roots.

Then, after having found their haunts, return some evening after dusk or some morning before sunrise for a good chance of seeing them.

MINK

Minks and weasels have long bodies, short legs, move in bounds or jumps.

SQUIRREL

Squirrels, in running, place hind feet in front of paired forefeet.

RABBIT

Rabbits bound like squirrels but place one forefoot behind other.

FIELD MOUSE

Mice and rats bound up and down, often show marks of dragging tail.

DEER

The tracks of members of the deer family show the sharp imprints of 2 hooves, in a heartlike pattern.

ANIMAL TRACKS

When you come upon an animal track, the first question you will ask yourself is probably, "What animal is it?" The next may be, "What was it doing?" And the third, "Where did it go?" Tracks on the ground are like words in a book—when you know how to read them, they'll tell you a story.

If you are just learning to track, let's hope you have timed the first lesson for a winter morning after a light flurry of snow. All tracks are clearly visible, especially if you look at them against a low sun. The shadows in the tracks will make them stand out sharply. But you may be living in a part of the country where there is no snow. In that case, the best place for finding and following tracks is along a lake or river shore.

The first tracks you will get to know will probably be those of your pet cat or dog. Look at those cat tracks: you see only the imprints of the soft pads, never of the claws. The same is the case of other members of the cat family: mountain lion, wildcat, cougar. The track of your dog, in contrast, shows clear claw marks. So do the tracks of other members of the dog family: fox, wolf, coyote.

Of wild animals, you will quickly learn to recognize the hoof marks of deer, the hand-

When galloping in mud or deep snow, the male deer may show marks of dewclaws in its tracks.

TRACK CAST— Negative

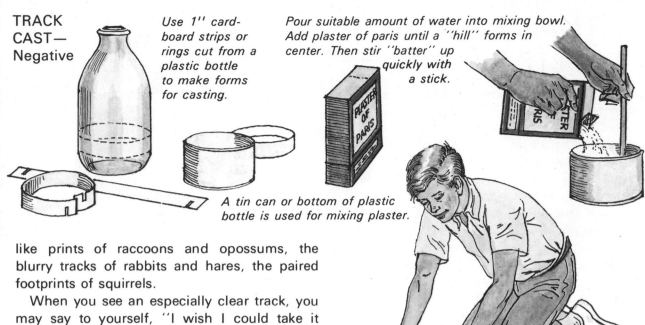

Use 1'' cardboard strips or rings cut from a plastic bottle to make forms for casting.

A tin can or bottom of plastic bottle is used for mixing plaster.

Pour suitable amount of water into mixing bowl. Add plaster of paris until a "hill" forms in center. Then stir "batter" up quickly with a stick.

like prints of raccoons and opossums, the blurry tracks of rabbits and hares, the paired footprints of squirrels.

When you see an especially clear track, you may say to yourself, "I wish I could take it home with me." You wouldn't have much luck digging it up. But there is a way of fulfilling your wish: you simply make a plaster cast of the track.

For this you need four things: 1) a white powder called plaster of paris, which you can buy in any paint store, 2) some plain water, 3) a container for mixing the plaster, 4) a few cardboard strips or plastic rings.

The procedure for making a cast is simple: You place a cardboard or plastic ring around the track to make a form, mix up a batch of plaster of paris, and pour it in. When set, you dig up the cast carefully.

This gives you a negative cast, with the track raised. If you desire a positive cast, with the track looking the way it appeared in the field, you use the negative as a form, and repeat the casting process.

Place cardboard or plastic ring around track to make a form for containing the plaster of paris batter.

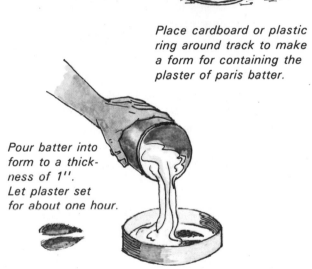

Pour batter into form to a thickness of 1''. Let plaster set for about one hour.

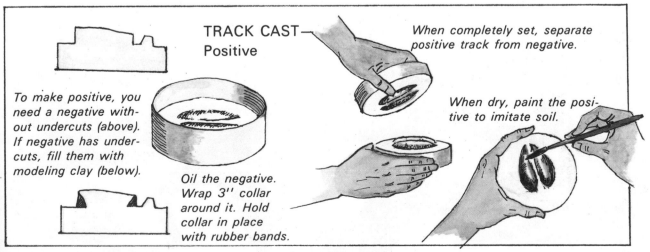

TRACK CAST— Positive

To make positive, you need a negative without undercuts (above). If negative has undercuts, fill them with modeling clay (below).

Oil the negative. Wrap 3'' collar around it. Hold collar in place with rubber bands.

When completely set, separate positive track from negative.

When dry, paint the positive to imitate soil.

SNAKES AND LIZARDS

Some day, on a hike across a field or meadow, you may see a movement in the grass in front of you. You suddenly realize that it must be a snake. But before you can take off after it, it has disappeared. "How is it possible," you may ask yourself, "for a creature without legs to move with such speed?" There is a special trick to it that all snakes have mastered: they glide along in sinuous curves, using the scales on the belly of their long bodies to grip the ground, and their scores of ribs and special muscles to carry them forward.

We have around two dozen different snake families in North America. Many of them make excellent pets; they are easy to keep in captivity and fun to handle. But, unfortunately, the snakes of four of the families are poisonous. So, before you take up snake collecting, you need to be able to identify our poisonous snakes so that you can evade them. Also, if your hiking takes you into areas that may be infested with poisonous snakes, you should always carry a snakebite kit.

By far the largest group of poisonous snakes is the one containing the rattlesnakes. They are found throughout North America. They are easily recognized by the horny, jointed rattle on the end of the tail. The copperheads occur in the eastern part of the country. They are copperish-brown, with hourglass-shaped crossbands of a darker color. The muddy-brown cottonmouth water moccasins live in southern streams and marshes. When they feel them-

Practiced snake collectors pick up nonpoisonous snakes with their hands and carry them home in cloth bags, with the top of the bags securely tied.

Strap stick for snake catching has a leather noose that runs in guides cut from tin can.

Simplest snake stick has a hook in one end.

POISONOUS SNAKES

Coral Snake

Cottonmouth

Copperhead

Diamondback Rattler

selves threatened, they raise their heads and open their mouths, showing the cotton-white inside. The coral snakes make up the last group. They are found in the Deep South but are seldom seen because they hunt only at night. They are brilliantly colored, with bands of coral-red, bright yellow, and black.

While studying snakes, you may become interested in studying lizards as well. Lizards are closely related to snakes. They may almost be considered snakes with legs. Most of the American species are found in dry, hot desert country. They are very hard to catch but, when once caught, make highly satisfactory pets.

If you decide to keep snakes or lizards in captivity, you can make a simple cage for them from wood and coarse wire mesh. Provide the cage with a water dish and with a few stones for a hiding place.

Snakes and lizards prefer live animal food. Small specimens can be fed earthworms and grubs. Larger snakes will take strips of meat but will definitely prefer live mice, served once a week.

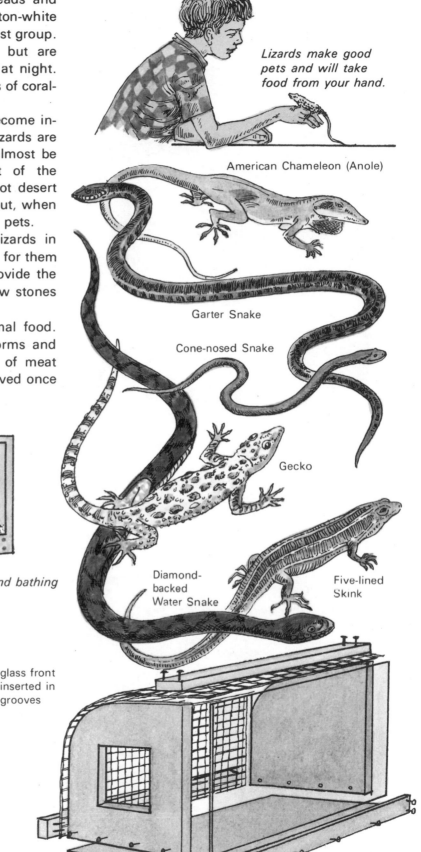

Lizards make good pets and will take food from your hand.

American Chameleon (Anole)

Garter Snake

Cone-nosed Snake

Gecko

Diamond-backed Water Snake

Five-lined Skink

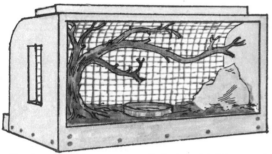

Snake cage has water dish for drinking and bathing and a few stones for hiding.

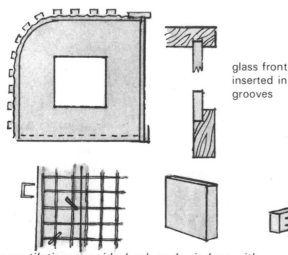

glass front inserted in grooves

For ventilation, provide back and window with coarse wire mesh.

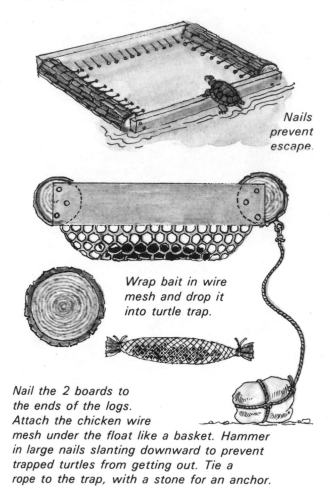

*Make a floating
turtle trap from 2 logs,
2 boards, some chicken wire.*

*Nails
prevent
escape.*

*Wrap bait in wire
mesh and drop it
into turtle trap.*

*Nail the 2 boards to
the ends of the logs.
Attach the chicken wire
mesh under the float like a basket. Hammer
in large nails slanting downward to prevent
trapped turtles from getting out. Tie a
rope to the trap, with a stone for an anchor.*

*The common snapper is a vicious animal. Never
keep a snapper as a pet. The jaws of even a
small snapper may cut off a person's finger.*

DANGEROUS

TURTLES FOR PETS

On a warm summer day, as you walk through the woods, you may notice the slow movement of an animal among the plants of the forest floor. You stop to investigate and discover that it is a turtle, an animal with its body enclosed in a shell—an upper, rounded part called a carapace, and a lower, rather flat part called a plastron. If the animal, on being disturbed, closes up its bottom shell completely, you know you have found a box turtle. If the animal has a deeply grooved upper shell, you have come upon a wood turtle.

Box turtles and wood turtles make excellent pets. You can keep them for a long time in a fenced-in pen in your yard or garden. Both of these kinds of turtles may eventually learn to take their food directly from your hand: fruits and berries, lettuce, earthworms and snails, various insects, chopped meat.

In addition to these land turtles, you may also have a chance to make pets out of small pond turtles.

Some hot day you may see some of these turtles sunning themselves on a log in a swamp, a quiet pond, or a slow-flowing stream. As you approach, they drop into the water and disappear. They are shy and not easily captured by hand. But they may be caught in a simple trap made from a couple of logs similar to those on which they sun themselves.

In the Northeast, the pond turtles you catch will probably be the painted or the spotted turtles that get to be about 6'' long. In the valleys of the Mississippi and its tributaries, they may be turtles belonging to a group called sliders that grow to a length of 1 foot. If you can't find any of these turtles in the wild, you may be able to buy them in a local pet shop. The larger ones of these turtles may be kept in an outdoor pen, as long as you sink some kind of basin into the ground and keep it supplied with water. The smaller ones you can keep in your home, in a terrarium also provided with a pan of water. Pond turtles get along on a diet of fish and scraps of meat, served in the water. As a matter of fact, a painted turtle can't swallow its food unless it has its head under water.

BOX TURTLE MAKES BEST PET

A box turtle makes an excellent pet. You can keep it in an outdoor pen or give it the run of the house. Box turtles may live to be 80 years old or older.

If the bottom shell is flat, your turtle is a female; if curved inward, it is a male.

Painted Turtle

Saw-toothed Slider

The small painted turtles (5'' to 6'') and the larger sliders (10'' to 12'') are excellent for a turtle terrarium. Feed them in the water.

TURTLE TERRARIUM is made the way you would make a woodland terrarium (see page 72), with a layer of dirt or sod on bottom. Put in a water pan level with the soil. Add a few stones and small plants.

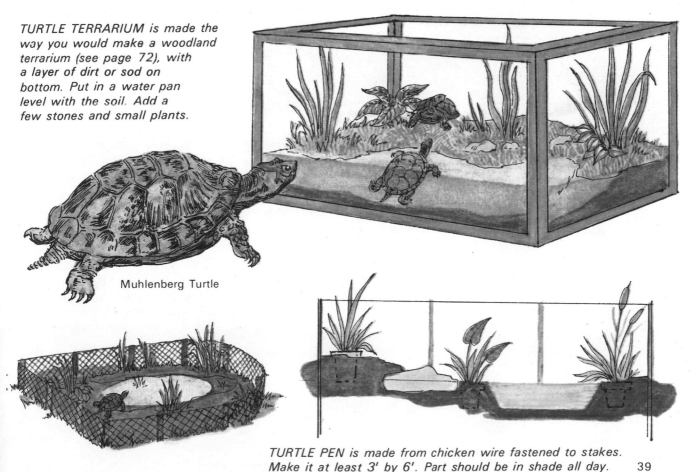

Muhlenberg Turtle

TURTLE PEN is made from chicken wire fastened to stakes. Make it at least 3' by 6'. Part should be in shade all day.   39

Frogs may be caught in several ways: by hand if you are quick enough (below), by fish hook baited with a piece of red cloth (left), by a 2-pronged spring attached to a stick. Check local conservation laws.

TOADS AND FROGS

To find toads and frogs aplenty, you'll have to go to meadows and swamplands, lakes and streams. These creatures are amphibious— from two Greek words: *amphi,* meaning "both sides," and *bios,* meaning "life." There are two sides to their lives. They spend the first part of life completely in the water, the rest on dry land and in and out of water.

Early in the spring, you can start looking for the eggs of toads and frogs in shallow ponds and sluggish streams. The eggs of toads come in long strings, those of frogs in masses like transparent tapioca pudding. Bring a few eggs home in a jar of water with a little plant matter. Place them on a cool window sill, then

Watch the development of toads and frogs from eggs through tadpole stage, to underwater creatures with 4 legs, into fully-grown amphibians.

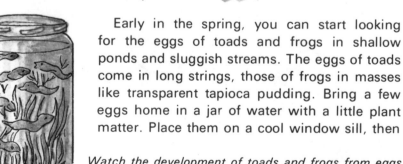

watch from day to day an amazing development.

Soon the dark center of each egg starts to grow and, in about a week, the eggs begin to hatch. Out come tiny tadpoles, less than an inch long. They do not look at all like toads or frogs. They have roundish heads and tails like tiny fish tails. They have no eyes and no mouth, only a sucking apparatus by which they can take nourishment.

In a few days you will notice tiny fringes growing out from the head of each tadpole. These are gills that make it possible for the tadpoles to breathe underwater, like fish. At the same time, eyes and a mouth develop. Before long, the outside gills grow over and the body gets bigger and more rounded. Then you will see two hind legs appear and, soon after, two front legs. At the same time, the tail begins to disappear. Inside, the tadpole develops lungs with which to breathe on land.

The time has come for you to transfer the tadpoles to a shallow aquarium that has a couple of stones reaching above the water for the young toads or frogs to climb as they turn into land animals. After that happens, you will have to decide whether you want to go on keeping a couple in a terrarium with a shallow water dish, feeding them regularly on mealworms, earthworms and slugs.

What's the difference between toads and frogs? Toads usually have warty skins and live on land. Frogs have smooth skin and live in wet places.

Spring Peeper

Fowler's Toad

Bullfrog

Leopard Frog

Tailed or Bell Toad

Terrarium for frogs needs a well-filled water dish.

diving mask

J-type snorkels

fins

For greatest enjoyment, go skin diving with snorkel for breathing, diving mask for viewing, fins for propulsion.

WATER LIFE

You have probably heard a couple of sayings comparing human beings with fish: "He swims like a fish." "He drinks like a fish."

"He swims like a fish" is a compliment—to the man—and a great overstatement. No man can swim like a fish for the simple reason that a fish is a special kind of creature, specifically suited to life in the water. Most fish have slim, streamlined bodies that permit them to speed through the water with little resistance. They have highly flexible backbones and powerful muscles that permit all kinds of movements.

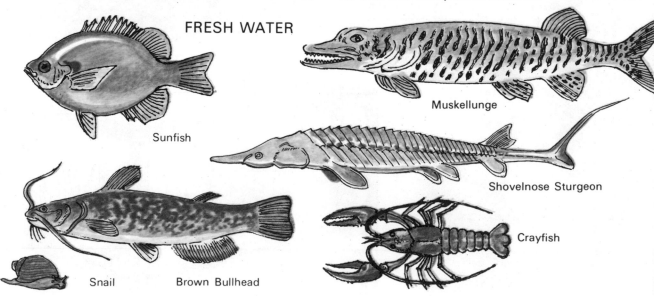

FRESH WATER

Sunfish

Muskellunge

Shovelnose Sturgeon

Snail

Brown Bullhead

Crayfish

They have two sets of paired fins that function like rowing oars and a tail efficient for sculling and steering. They have air bladders they can fill for raising or lowering their bodies in the water.

"He drinks like a fish" is an insult—to the fish. No fish drinks excessively although it may look that way. When a fish has its mouth wide open for taking in a great amount of water, it is not for drinking it, but for breathing and feeding. The water contains oxygen that is absorbed in the fish's gills. And it contains great amounts of nourishing plant and animal life as well.

If you live inland, you can study fish life in any clear-water lake or pond. If you live along one of our shores, you have the ocean or gulf for your study.

And then, when once you have picked up an interest in water life by studying the fish of fresh or salt water, you may want to extend your study to other kinds of water life: to crabs and lobsters, mussels and oysters, starfish and jellyfish, worms and sponges, and many other animals that inhabit salt water; or to amphibians and reptiles, crayfish and leeches, snails and clams, and lots and lots of other forms of freshwater life.

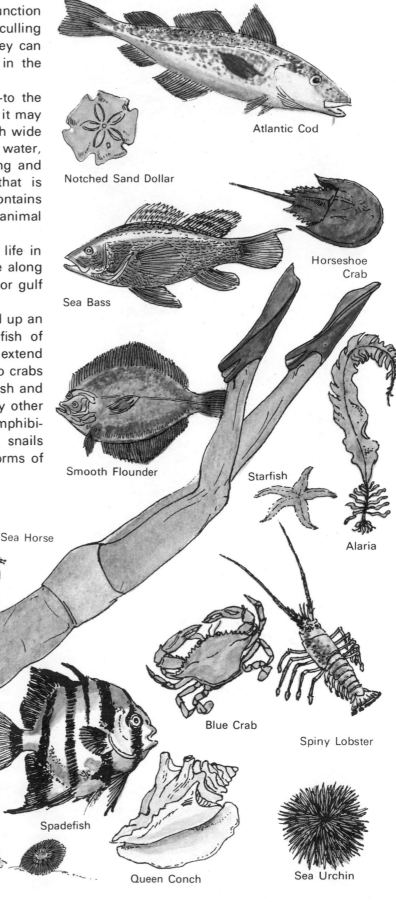

Atlantic Cod

Notched Sand Dollar

Horseshoe Crab

Sea Bass

Smooth Flounder

Starfish

Alaria

SALT WATER

Sea Horse

Pinfish

Coral

Spadefish

Blue Crab

Spiny Lobster

Anemone

Queen Conch

Sea Urchin

AQUATIC EXPLORING

For complete exploration and investigation of a lake or an ocean shore, you need a few pieces of special equipment.

The first item is a gadget for looking down into the water without having to get in and out all the time. The difficulty of seeing from above what is in the water is caused by the fact that the water's surface acts like a mirror and reflects the sky. To eliminate this reflection, you have to get below the surface. This can be done with a waterscope—a waterproof box or tube with a transparent bottom of plexiglass or regular glass. After putting the glass bottom of the scope in the water, you can look down into the scope and now see clearly everything that is in the water. The view will be even better if you paint the inside of the scope black.

For the complete investigation of a shallow lake or the shore of the sea, it will be necessary for you to bring samples of whatever ani-

For catching small water creatures, use a dip net. A kitchen wire strainer will do the job. Or make a net similar to the insect net on page 62.

Many water creatures of a tidal pool (left) are particularly active at night. Hunt them with a flashlight. Have bucket with water ready for them.

Make a scraper net from tough netting. Reinforce edge with muslin. Sew onto D-shaped wire frame that has straight edge as long as the rake you'll use.

For working shallows and shorelines, make a rigid apron net from wire mesh. Attach an iron bar along bottom front edge to hold it down. Pull it slowly.

Attach scraper net to rake and rake handle with wires.

mal life is there out of the water or up from the bottom. Small animals swimming in the water, such as tiny fish, tadpoles, insects and insect larvas, can be caught with a dip net. Snails and crabs may be brought out of a tidal pool by hand. Water life that moves about on the bottom of a lake or hangs onto water plants may be caught in an apron net pulled behind a boat. For animals that dig themselves into the sand along the shore or into the muck of a tidal flat, you can use a scraper net.

Whatever animals you find, throw them immediately into a bucket of water to keep them alive. If you are just making a survey of water life, you can now make a list of the animals and return them to the water. On the other hand, if you are planning to stock an aquarium or to add to your water life collection, pick out the better specimens and throw the rest back.

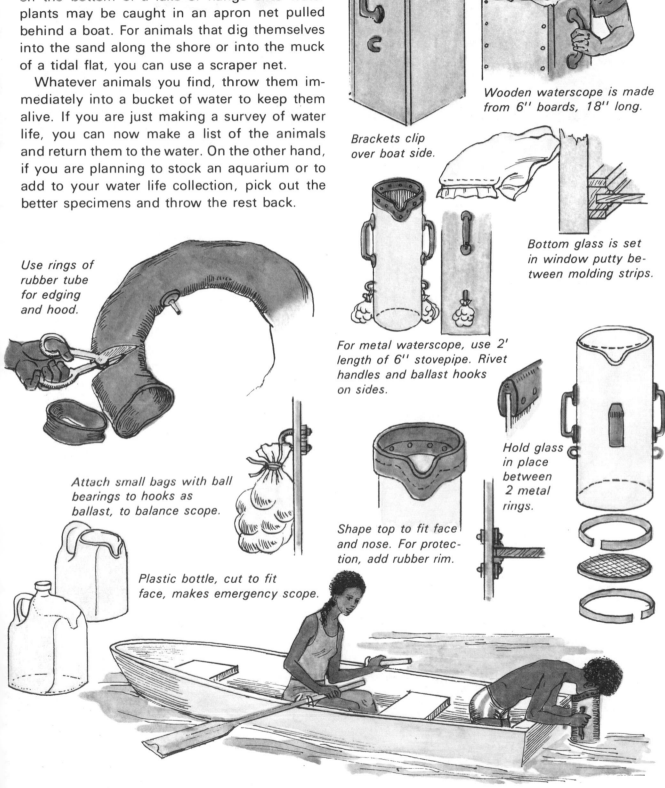

Wooden waterscope is made from 6'' boards, 18'' long.

Brackets clip over boat side.

Bottom glass is set in window putty between molding strips.

Use rings of rubber tube for edging and hood.

For metal waterscope, use 2' length of 6'' stovepipe. Rivet handles and ballast hooks on sides.

Hold glass in place between 2 metal rings.

Attach small bags with ball bearings to hooks as ballast, to balance scope.

Shape top to fit face and nose. For protection, add rubber rim.

Plastic bottle, cut to fit face, makes emergency scope.

FRESHWATER AQUARIUM

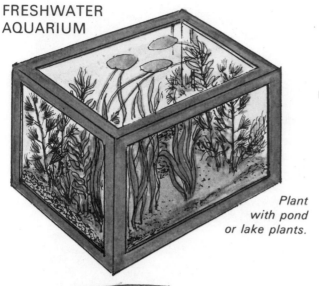

Plant with pond or lake plants.

FRESHWATER LIFE

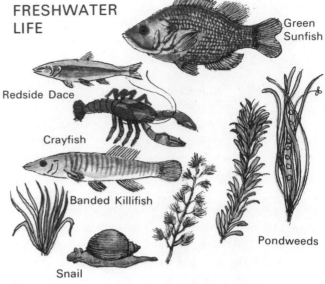

Green Sunfish

Redside Dace

Crayfish

Banded Killifish

Pondweeds

Snail

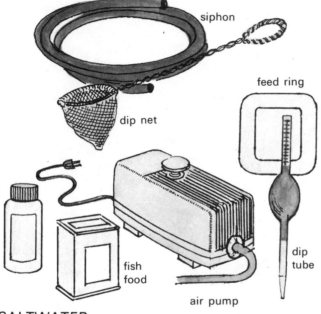

siphon

dip net

feed ring

fish food

air pump

dip tube

MAKING AN AQUARIUM

One of these days, you may decide to become an "aquarist"—one of the millions of happy hobbyists who go in for establishing and maintaining aquariums for the fun of watching fish in their natural element while, at the same time, adding an attractive decoration and a conversation piece to their living rooms.

For most hobbies, the rule is "start small." Not when establishing an aquarium. Here it is a matter of starting as large, within reason, as you can afford and have room for. Your minimum should be a 5-gallon aquarium tank. Even more satisfactory would be a tank of 10-gallon

SALTWATER AQUARIUM

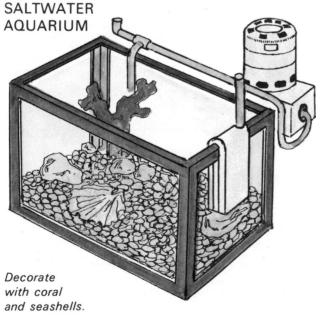

Decorate with coral and seashells.

SALTWATER LIFE

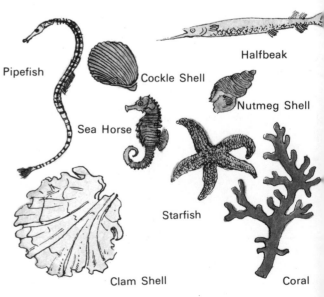

Pipefish

Cockle Shell

Halfbeak

Nutmeg Shell

Sea Horse

Starfish

Clam Shell

Coral

capacity or more. Place the tank in a part of the room where it will get diffused light throughout the day and where it can be easily illuminated by artificial light.

To make a freshwater aquarium truly attractive, it should contain a few water plants. They are valuable also for providing shelter for the more timid fish, a repository for eggs, hiding places for babies, food for certain types of fish. These plants will require something in which to anchor. So your first concern is to secure some coarse river sand or fine gravel. Wash it thoroughly in clean water, then place a layer of it in the bottom of the tank, slanting it from one end to the other so that food remnants may drift to the lower end for easy removal with a dip tube. Fill the tank part way with water, and plant in the sand a few local water plants you have collected in a nearby pond or lake. Fill up the tank. When the water has settled, introduce the fish.

The majority of aquarists go in for exotic fish and buy them in a pet store. You will have far more fun if you stick to native fish and catch them yourself. Shiners and minnows, darters and killifish, sticklebacks and sunfish, are all suitable for your native aquarium. The red-bellied and the black-nosed daces are particularly desirable. In addition to a variety of small fish, include a few snails. Snails are scavengers—they will help keep your aquarium clean.

When it comes to feeding, you should be able to scoop the natural food out of the same pond where you caught your fish. Otherwise, purchase regular aquarium food.

If your choice is a saltwater aquarium rather than a freshwater, the procedure of establishing it is pretty much the same, with one difference: no plants. If you want some kind of decoration, use pieces of coral or a few sea-shells. It should be possible for you to get the fish and other water life you want from a small tidal pool.

One thing is of extreme importance for the saltwater aquarium: that the water be thoroughly aerated. Saltwater fish need a great deal more oxygen than freshwater fish. You will therefore have to install an air pump that will pump air into an air stone placed close to the bottom of the tank from which the air will bubble through the water.

ESTABLISHING THE FRESHWATER AQUARIUM

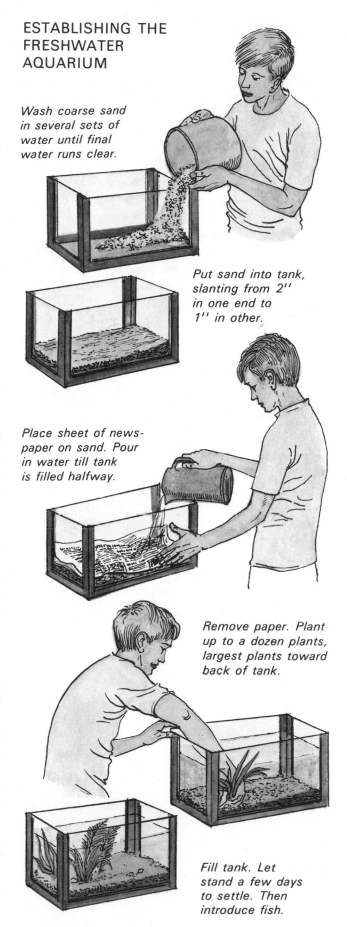

Wash coarse sand in several sets of water until final water runs clear.

Put sand into tank, slanting from 2" in one end to 1" in other.

Place sheet of newspaper on sand. Pour in water till tank is filled halfway.

Remove paper. Plant up to a dozen plants, largest plants toward back of tank.

Fill tank. Let stand a few days to settle. Then introduce fish.

GOING FISHING

The best excuse for studying fish life is "going fishing." "Going fishing" is one of the finest forms of recreation. It gets you out in the open. It fills your hours with expectation. It teaches you patience. It provides you with some very special thrills each time a finny "denizen of the deep" grabs your lure.

In the beginning, even the simplest cane-pole outfit will do, with the old-time earthworm on your hook.

But you will probably want to graduate as quickly as possible to bait casting, fly casting, and spin casting. To have success with these methods, you need to know your fish, their haunts, and their habits, as well as the proper kind of equipment.

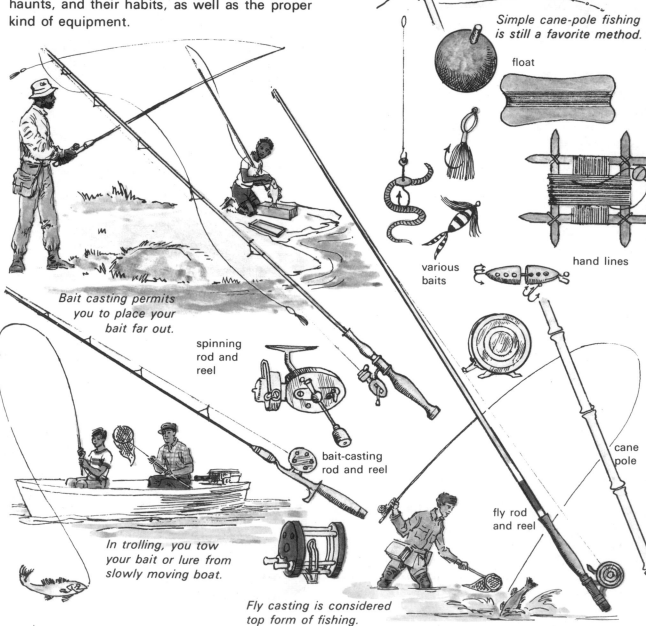

Simple cane-pole fishing is still a favorite method.

float

various baits

hand lines

Bait casting permits you to place your bait far out.

spinning rod and reel

bait-casting rod and reel

cane pole

In trolling, you tow your bait or lure from slowly moving boat.

fly rod and reel

Fly casting is considered top form of fishing.

To make a cast of a fish, make a bottomless box of a size to fit your fish. Fill half with sand. Push fish halfway into sand. Pour in plaster of paris batter. Let set.

Lift up box, letting fish and sand fall out. Turn the box over. The negative cast will stay in it. Brush the negative with mineral oil. Pour in plaster of paris batter. Let set.

When completely dry, separate positive from negative. For better likeness, paint the positive with oil paints. Use negative for making more positives.

MAKING FISH CASTS AND FISH PRINTS

Some time in the future, you may become a deep-sea fisherman, setting out on a charter boat into the Gulf Stream off the coast of Florida or into some corner of the Caribbean Sea. And perhaps, with some good luck, you will catch a sailfish or a marlin or some other giant of the sea—as some fishermen do. And so you will probably do what other deep-sea fishermen do—you will want to have your trophy mounted to prove your prowess in angling. That job is a task for an expert taxidermist. It may cost you a few hundred dollars—but, by then, you may find it worth

while—that is, if you have a wall on which to display your trophy.

But before that dream of the future comes true, you may want to make a record of the fish you have caught, even if it isn't of giant proportions. To do this, you can do what some people do: make a plaster cast of your prize catch. Or you can do what some other people do: make an ink print of it.

For the plaster cast, you need sand and a casting form and the plaster of paris batter described on page 35. For the fish print, you can use regular India ink, Japanese *sumi* ink, or diluted poster paint in a color you like. You will further need a broad brush, some sheets of tissue or rice paper, and a rubbing cloth.

With some care, your fish casts or fish prints should turn out very well indeed and be a worthy exhibit on one of your walls.

To make a fish print, start by rubbing fish dry with salt. Then paint it quickly with ink or diluted poster paint. Place a sheet of tissue or rice paper over fish, cover with a piece of cloth, and rub carefully, until all inked areas have been transferred to tissue paper. Remove paper carefully. Let dry. When completely dry, retouch, mount on cardboard.

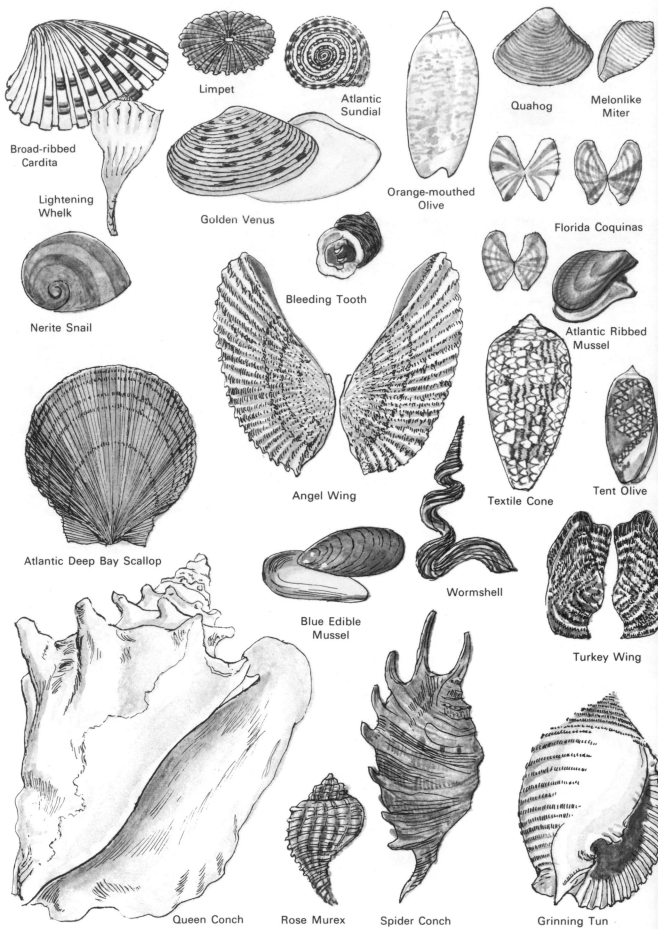

Broad-ribbed
Cardita

Limpet

Atlantic
Sundial

Quahog

Melonlike
Miter

Lightening
Whelk

Orange-mouthed
Olive

Golden Venus

Florida Coquinas

Nerite Snail

Bleeding Tooth

Atlantic Ribbed
Mussel

Atlantic Deep Bay Scallop

Angel Wing

Textile Cone

Tent Olive

Blue Edible
Mussel

Wormshell

Turkey Wing

Queen Conch

Rose Murex

Spider Conch

Grinning Tun

A rake or a small spade will help you uncover mollusks that hide in the sand.

SEASHELLS

The seashells you find along the shore are the remains of a group of animals known as "mollusks." After the insects, this group contains more different species than any other subdivision of animal life. It has the further distinction of containing some of the earliest creatures that ever lived. Fossils of mollusk shells have been found in rocks formed more than 500,000,000 years ago.

Mollusks get their name from a Latin word that means "soft." They all have soft bodies and no bones whatever. Almost all of them are protected by a hard shell. Some of them, such as periwinkles, cowries, whelks, and conches, have a single, spirally-twisted shell. A great number of others have two matching shells that can be closed up tight by a special muscle. Some of these two-shelled mollusks have provided food for people from the very beginning of human existence: oysters, clams, scallops, mussels.

Many collectors add to their collection by purchase or swapping.

For collecting in shallow water (far left), float a basket in the water. For collecting in deep water, float inflated tire on the water, with net for your loot, and stone anchor.

SHELL COLLECTING

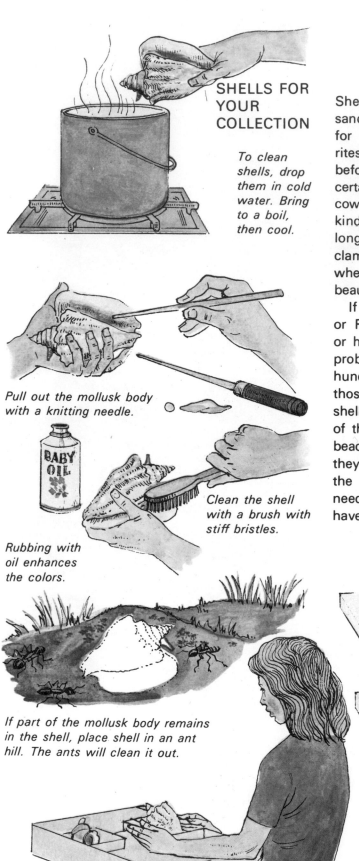

SHELLS FOR YOUR COLLECTION

To clean shells, drop them in cold water. Bring to a boil, then cool.

Pull out the mollusk body with a knitting needle.

Clean the shell with a brush with stiff bristles.

Rubbing with oil enhances the colors.

If part of the mollusk body remains in the shell, place shell in an ant hill. The ants will clean it out.

Put the shells in cardboard boxes and arrange them in your drawers.

Shell collecting has been going on for thousands of years. Many ancient tribes used shells for jewels and decorations and in religious rites. The early Egyptians made use of shells before our kind of money was invented—a certain shell they used is still called a "money cowrie." The American Indians had their own kind of money in the form of "wampum"—oblong beads carved from the shell of the quahog clam or made from the core of the knobbed whelk. Today people collect shells for their beauty and their fascinating structure.

If you live near the shores of the Atlantic or Pacific Oceans or of the Gulf of Mexico, or have had occasion to visit them, you have probably already picked up shells by the hundreds, some of them the shells of bivalves—those mollusks that have two parts to their shells—others the single, cone-shaped shells of the marine snails. But shells found on the beach are seldom suitable for a collection—they will be wave-worn and chipped along the edges. For a worthwhile collection you need perfect specimens. To get them you will have to go hunting for the live animals in the

Identify and label your specimen.

For attractive display and safe handling, you can glue specimens onto blocks of styrofoam.

Keep tiny shells in plastic containers meant for coins—dimes, quarters, half-dollars.

sand of a beach, in the mud of a mud flat, on the bottom of the sea right off the shore, among the rocks of a tidal pool, on the wooden or concrete supports of a pier or wharf.

The best area of shore or mud flat for finding mollusks is the section between the high and the low water marks. The best time is when the tide is going out. As you walk along the shore or in the mud flat, the vibrations from your footsteps will warn the mollusks. They will want to dig themselves deeper into their burrows. As they do this, they squirt up a jet of water from their holes. If you dig quickly with a small spade, you will have a chance to catch them.

If you are a good swimmer, you can pick up mollusks from the bottom of the sea. Put on goggles and snorkel and fins and swim slowly along the coastline. Watch for trails in the sand that will lead you to your prey, then dive down and pick up your specimens. Place them in a mesh bag attached to a belt around your waist.

When hunting for shells in a tidal pool, be sure to wear sneakers or tennis shoes to prevent your feet from being cut by barnacles or by the sharp edges of shells.

After finding your specimens, you proceed to clean them. This is generally done by boiling them, then scraping loose the muscle, if a bivalve, or pulling the body out of the shell, if a marine snail. The cleaned shells are then dried, identified, put in suitable boxes, labeled, and placed in your collection.

SHELLS FOR DECORATION

Use a good guide book for identifying your specimens.

Conch shell makes an interesting flower container.

Enclose extra-fine specimen in glass box or embed in plastic.

A single large shell mounted on a pedestal or a number of shells arranged together will make an attractive table decoration.

Tiny shells can be turned into fine jewelry.

53

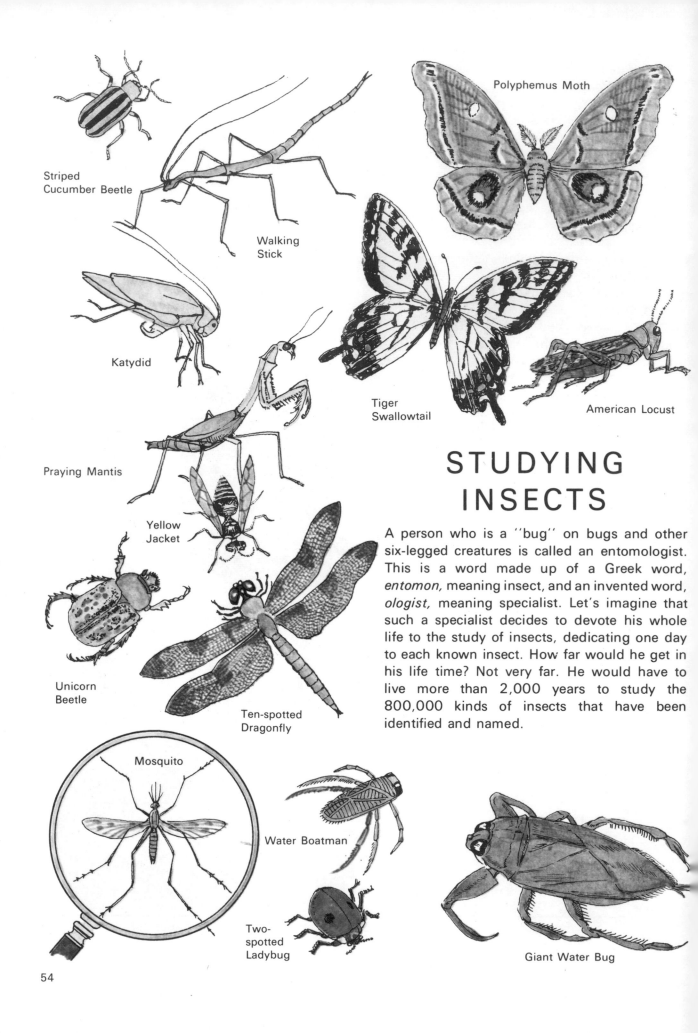

Striped
Cucumber Beetle

Walking
Stick

Polyphemus Moth

Katydid

Tiger
Swallowtail

American Locust

Praying Mantis

Yellow
Jacket

Unicorn
Beetle

Ten-spotted
Dragonfly

STUDYING
INSECTS

A person who is a ''bug'' on bugs and other six-legged creatures is called an entomologist. This is a word made up of a Greek word, *entomon,* meaning insect, and an invented word, *ologist,* meaning specialist. Let's imagine that such a specialist decides to devote his whole life to the study of insects, dedicating one day to each known insect. How far would he get in his life time? Not very far. He would have to live more than 2,000 years to study the 800,000 kinds of insects that have been identified and named.

Mosquito

Water Boatman

Two-
spotted
Ladybug

Giant Water Bug

54

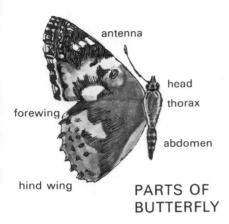

antenna

head

thorax

abdomen

forewing

hind wing

PARTS OF BUTTERFLY

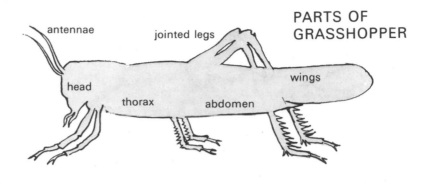

antennae

jointed legs

PARTS OF GRASSHOPPER

head

thorax

abdomen

wings

So don't bite off too large a bite if you should become interested in the study of insects. Start off by getting to know some of the more important groups or orders and some of the more familiar insects within each order.

To do this you will need certain equipment for collecting insects and some for the close study of them. For their identification you will require good insect books—a simple one to start with, such as a Golden Nature Guide, and a more complete field book later on.

In each of these books, the insects are arranged according to the orders to which they belong. The knowledge of a bit of scientific lingo will help you identify an insect you see.

More than half of all insect orders have Latin names of Greek origin that end with *ptera* which means wings. So when you study a flying insect you have caught, take a good look at its wings. If they are covered with tiny scales—*lepido* in Latinized Greek—the insect belongs to the order of lepidoptera and is a butterfly or a moth. If the wings are like hard sheaths—*coleo*—the insect is a member of the coleoptera order: the beetles.

You can figure out the names of several other orders of insects when you know the word for the kind of wings they have: straight, *ortho* (grasshoppers and crickets); membranelike, *hymeno* (bees and wasps); hard and membranelike—half and half—*hemi* (bugs). While adult insects of these orders have four wings, flies have only two, *di*, giving their order the name of *diptera*.

Add to these orders one more order of flying insects, the dragonflies—*odonata*—and you are able to fit into their orders, for identification, the vast majority of insects you find.

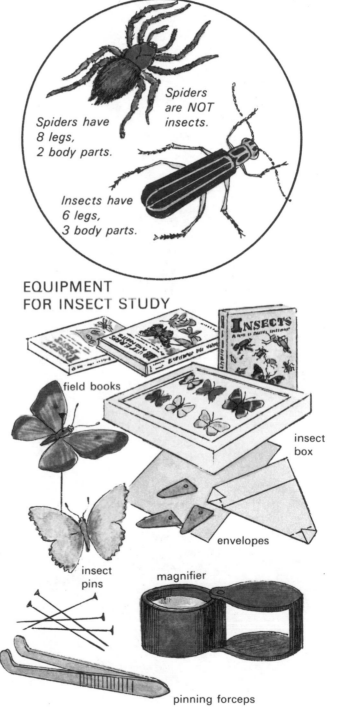

Spiders are NOT insects.

Spiders have 8 legs, 2 body parts.

Insects have 6 legs, 3 body parts.

EQUIPMENT FOR INSECT STUDY

field books

insect box

envelopes

insect pins

magnifier

pinning forceps

FINDING INSECTS

You will have no problem finding insects. The moment you step outdoors there are insects all around you. It's a matter of knowing where to look and what to look for. And just in case you are not actually trying to find *them,* they will find *you.*

Remember the summer day you went on a picnic with your family? You had hardly spread out your food before a fly sat down on the hamburger, a bee hovered over the jelly sandwich, a hornet drowned itself in your orange drink, a dozen ants crawled onto your cake.

These insects were all flying or crawling adults. But insects come in many other forms.

With very few exceptions, insects start their life as tiny eggs laid on leaves or on tree branches, in flowers or in plant stems, in fruits or in roots, on living animals or in rotting carcasses, in the ground or in the water. From this point on, insects turn into adults in different ways.

Some of the "higher" insects—moths, butterflies, beetles, wasps, ants, bees, flies—come out of their eggs as larvas that don't look at all the way the adult insects will look. These larvas may be leaf-eating caterpillars, root-eating grubs, maggots feeding on dead animal or plant matter. When these larvas have reached their maximum size, they turn into pupas, hiding in some plant part or in the unshed larval skin or in a cocoon. From these pupas eventually emerge the adult insects.

Some insects—grasshoppers and dragonflies, for instance—skip the pupa stage in their development. They emerge from their eggs in the form of "nymphs." Grasshopper nymphs resemble the adults but have no wings. They shed their skin several times as they grow in size, finally coming out of a molt with completely developed wings. The nymphs of dragonflies are unlike the adults. They are born underwater and grow up in the water, breathing with gills. When they have reached their full size, they crawl out of the water, break their skin, and fly off as fully developed dragonflies.

So, for complete insect study, it is not just a matter of looking for the adults, but also of finding them in all their other forms.

For a simple light-trap, focus a flashlight beam against a sheet hung in a tree. Spread out edge of sheet to catch exhausted insects.

CAPTURING INSECTS

Many of the daytime insects you may want to study you will have to go hunting for, catching them on the wing. Insects that are about in the nighttime, on the other hand, may be tricked into letting themselves be captured.

Most night-flying insects—particularly small and large moths—are attracted to bright light. So rig up a light source and wait for the insects to come flying. They will continue circling until they finally drop down, exhausted, in whatever receptacle you have waiting.

Moths and other night fliers may also be captured by luring them with a tasty bait painted on as many tree trunks as you have bait to go around. For bait you can use a heavy molasses or the pulp from overripe fruit mixed with sugar—brown sugar, preferably.

The same sweet bait can also be used for capturing crawling insects. Simply sink a tin can or other container into the ground and pour in a small amount.

There is still another bait that is highly effective, especially with certain beetles. You wouldn't like it—but they do. This bait is a small piece of meat gone bad or a piece of fish gone putrid. For capturing this kind of beetle, you can't beat a dead mouse!

A sweet bait dabbed on a tree will attract many night fliers.

If you can hang up a naked bulb, suspend it over a funnel cut from a plastic bottle with a jar below.

A box with a light bulb inside and one side replaced with 2 pieces of glass makes a good light-trap.

Many beetles like putrid flesh—carrion. A wire-mesh funnel will keep insects from escaping.

Cover bait can with piece of plywood against rain.

Sweet bait is effective in a can sunk in the ground.

57

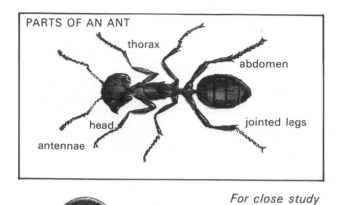

PARTS OF AN ANT

thorax

abdomen

head

jointed legs

antennae

INSECT HOMES

Some of the important insect families are truly "families." The insects live together and work together in big underground homes, in hollow trees, or in large hanging "palaces."

With the exception of the destructive termites, these "social insects" all belong to the order of hymenoptera—"the membrane-winged ones."

ANTS There are probably more individual ants in the world than of any other kind of creatures. They rank in size from the ferocious fire ants to ants so small you can hardly see them.

When you come upon a colony of ants— usually in the form of an anthill—take plenty of time to study them as they come rushing home with food or building materials. If you stir up a small section of the hill with a stick, all activity is speeded up tremendously as the ants run about, bringing their pupas—mistakenly called "ant eggs"—to safety.

Ants make excellent pets. By making a house for them out of scrap wood and two sheets of glass you can keep them at home and can study their activities at leisure.

For close study of ants, use a strong magnifier.

Most native ants live in hills that contain many galleries.

In collecting ants for your ant house, aim to catch the queen besides getting workers, larvas, pupas.

1"

5/8"

Circles of tin can cover holes in top.

9½"

10"

14"

6"

2"

To feed, place small sponges under 2 holes.

Drip water on one sponge, drops of diluted honey on other. Feed flies, aphids by third hole.

Make U-shaped frame and top from ½" stock. Use glass for sides. Glue or tape together.

When you are not watching, darken the sides with cardboard.

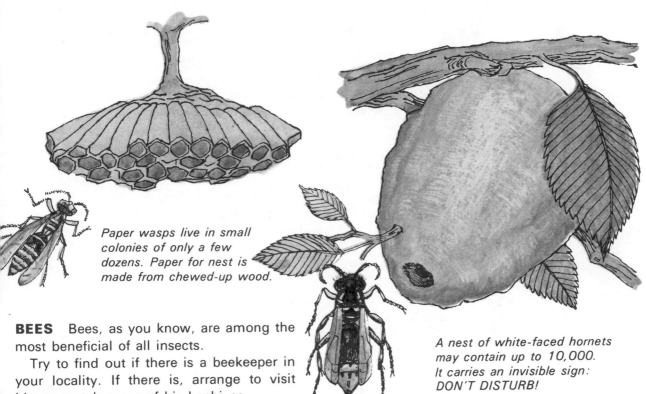

Paper wasps live in small colonies of only a few dozens. Paper for nest is made from chewed-up wood.

BEES Bees, as you know, are among the most beneficial of all insects.

Try to find out if there is a beekeeper in your locality. If there is, arrange to visit him to watch some of his beehives.

WASPS Wasps were making paper for constructing their homes thousands of years before the Chinese invented our kind of paper.

You can study the life of paper wasps without danger as they fly back and forth to their nest. But don't get too close to the large hanging nest of the bald-faced or white-faced hornet: the hornets may attack you.

A nest of white-faced hornets may contain up to 10,000. It carries an invisible sign: DON'T DISTURB!

HORNET NEST makes a spectacular display, but collect only after frost has killed off the insects. Bring home in a plastic bag.

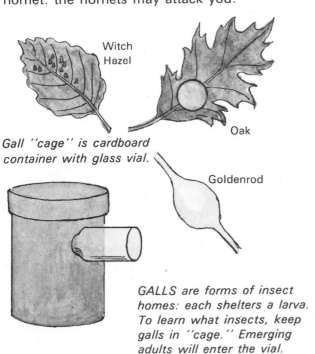

Witch Hazel

Oak

Gall "cage" is cardboard container with glass vial.

Goldenrod

GALLS are forms of insect homes: each shelters a larva. To learn what insects, keep galls in "cage." Emerging adults will enter the vial.

To be safe, spray with insecticide to kill possible survivors.

Cut off branch to which nest is attached.

INSECT SPRAY

Use pieces of slab wood for mounting the nest.

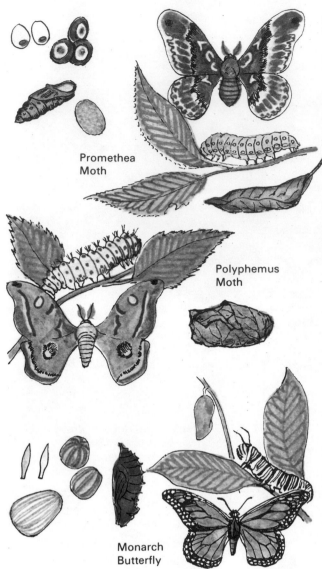

Promethea Moth

Polyphemus Moth

Monarch Butterfly

RASING INSECTS

Sooner or later, you will want to follow the whole life cycle of an insect, from its egg to its adult form. This is particularly interesting in the cases of butterflies and moths. It is quite easily done, as long as you know a bit of botany and have a lot of patience.

In studying your insect book, you will find that the larvas—caterpillars—of certain butterflies and moths feed on certain specific plants: monarch butterflies on milkweed, for instance, luna moths on sweet gum trees, walnut, and hickory, sphinx moths on several garden plants such as tomato and lilac.

The trick is to know these plants and to look for eggs or caterpillars on them in spring and early summer, and for pupas attached to them, or on the ground below, in the fall.

If you find the single eggs of some butterflies or the egg masses of some moths, bring them home, place them in a jar, and wait for the larvas to emerge. When this happens you need to get busy. Caterpillars have a voracious appetite and eat only the kind of plants on which the eggs were found. Bring in some of these plants, put them in water in a vase or in a jar to keep fresh, and place the larvas on the leaves. To keep the larvas within bound, surround everything with a plastic bag. Replace the plants that wilt.

With a good magnifying glass you can study the designs of insect eggs.

Regal Moth

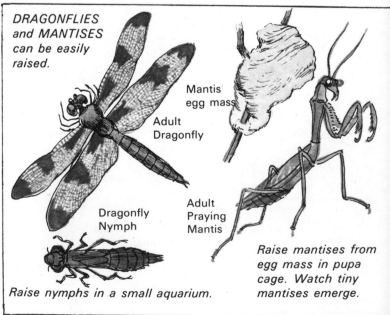

DRAGONFLIES and MANTISES can be easily raised.

Adult Dragonfly

Mantis egg mass

Adult Praying Mantis

Dragonfly Nymph

Raise nymphs in a small aquarium.

Raise mantises from egg mass in pupa cage. Watch tiny mantises emerge.

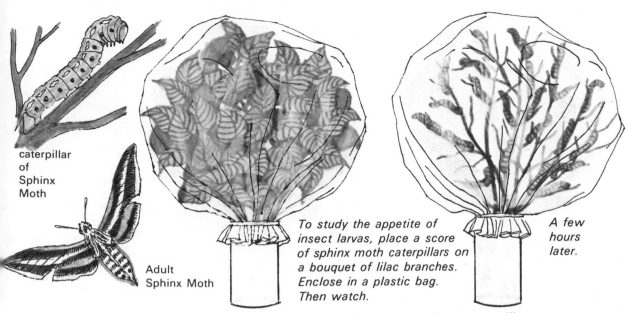

caterpillar
of
Sphinx
Moth

Adult
Sphinx Moth

To study the appetite of insect larvas, place a score of sphinx moth caterpillars on a bouquet of lilac branches. Enclose in a plastic bag. Then watch.

A few hours later.

Eventually, the caterpillars will turn into pupas: silk-covered cocoons of moths, naked chrysalises of butterflies. This is where your patience comes in. Nature takes her time for turning a pupa into an adult insect. In the open, a pupa generally spends the winter attached to a branch or lying on the ground until spring of the following year. The closest you can come to imitating nature is to keep your pupas in the hydrator of your refrigerator.

In the spring, when the feed plants of the particular insects have formed leaves, bring out the pupas and keep them in a pupa cage until the adult insects emerge. Then free the adults to fly off to start a new generation of their kind.

The appetite of tent caterpillars— the larvas of the Malacosoma moth— can be studied in the open. Transfer a dozen larvas from the "tent" to the tip of a branch. Place plastic bag over them and tie.

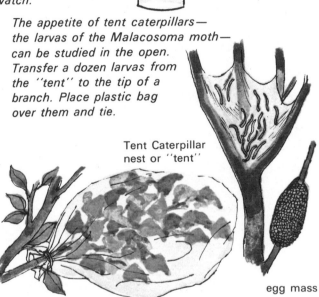

Tent Caterpillar
nest or "tent"

egg mass

PUPA CAGES

Make a cage from a plastic cottage cheese container or a paper bag. Provide it with window of clear plastic.

Place cocoon or chrysalis on dirt layer or attached to a stick. Put in wad of moistened cotton to keep from drying out.

DRAGONFLIES

Keep dragonfly nymphs in a large glass of water covered with a saucer, or in one small plastic aquarium covered with another.

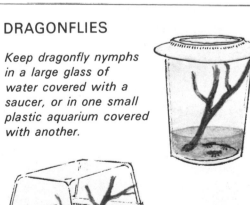

Place a stick for emerging adult dragonflies to cling to.

In "sweeping" (left), you swing a sweeping net through grass and weeds to pick up the insects hiding there. In "air netting" (right), you use an air net for catching butterflies and moths as they settle down on some flower.

When beating insects off the branches of a bush, catch them in an umbrella or a beating cloth tied to 2 sticks.

12"

frame

air net

10"

24"

12"

sweeping net

edging

19"

28"

tape

Air net (top) is made by sewing 4 narrow pieces of netting together, sweeping net (middle) by using 2 wider pieces of cloth.

beating cloth

HUNTING FOR INSECTS

Your main "weapons" for hunting insects are two nets: one for sweeping back and forth through grasses and weeds for catching-as-catch-can, the other for the more exciting adventure of air netting butterflies "on the wing" or, rather, on the flowers on which they settle down to feed.

The net for sweeping should be made of tough cotton or nylon cloth. Cut two pieces, about 19" by 28". Round the bottoms. Sew the pieces together into a bag. Open two wire clothes hangers and shape them into circles. Tape them together with friction tape or rubber tape into a stiff frame. Sew the net onto the frame. Finish off by providing the net with a reinforcement edge of cloth. Attach the net to a piece of dowel stick or old broomstick by the method shown.

The net for air netting can be made to the same pattern and in the same way as the sweeping net. But for this you use a mesh netting in place of cloth, preferably of nylon or Dacron. A slightly better net results by using four narrow pieces, 10" wide by 24" long, pointed at the bottom.

The technique for sweeping is very simple: you just swing the net back and forth, with the opening foremost, over and through grasses and weeds, picking up whatever insects are there. Your catch may contain anything from bugs to beetles, from grasshoppers to leafhoppers, from ants to flies. Dump the catch into your killing jar. Sort out the different insects after you get home.

The technique for air netting of butterflies is far more sophisticated—it is a true hunt. It begins with finding a suitable hunting area—some place where flowers that attract butterflies, such as milkweed and butterfly weed, honeysuckle and bee balm, grow in profusion. When you have located the spot, keep your eyes on one specific butterfly and make up your mind to catch it. You don't do this by pursuing it wildly across the field. Instead, you wait for it to settle on a flower for taking in nourishment by sucking up nectar. When it is well settled and relaxed, a quick sweep with your net will get it.

Killing jar uses nail polish remover on cotton covered with blotting paper or wired onto inside of lid.

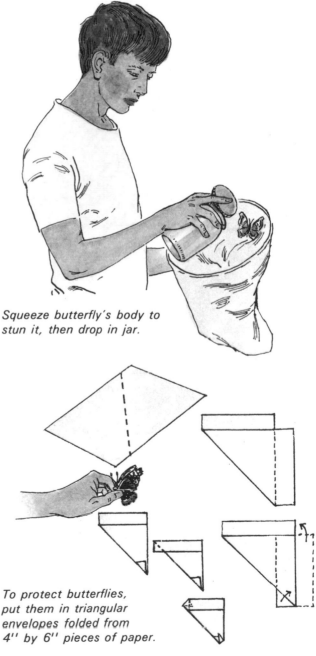

Squeeze butterfly's body to stun it, then drop in jar.

To protect butterflies, put them in triangular envelopes folded from 4" by 6" pieces of paper.

SPREADING BOARD

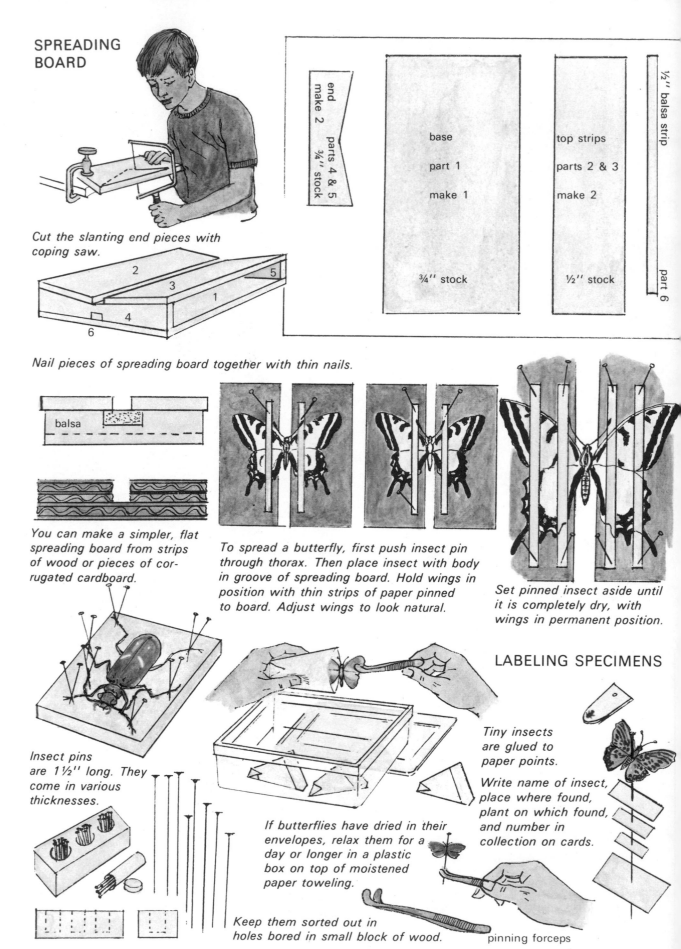

Cut the slanting end pieces with coping saw.

end
parts 4 & 5
make 2
¾'' stock

base

part 1

make 1

¾'' stock

top strips

parts 2 & 3

make 2

½'' stock

½'' balsa strip

part 6

Nail pieces of spreading board together with thin nails.

balsa

You can make a simpler, flat spreading board from strips of wood or pieces of corrugated cardboard.

To spread a butterfly, first push insect pin through thorax. Then place insect with body in groove of spreading board. Hold wings in position with thin strips of paper pinned to board. Adjust wings to look natural.

Set pinned insect aside until it is completely dry, with wings in permanent position.

LABELING SPECIMENS

Insect pins are 1½'' long. They come in various thicknesses.

If butterflies have dried in their envelopes, relax them for a day or longer in a plastic box on top of moistened paper toweling.

Keep them sorted out in holes bored in small block of wood.

Tiny insects are glued to paper points.

Write name of insect, place where found, plant on which found, and number in collection on cards.

pinning forceps

MAKING A RIKER MOUNT

Cut lid of box in shape of a frame.

cotton batting

moth crystals

MOTH CRYSTAL

Keep glass in place with adhesive tape.

box lid

glass

INSECT BOXES

A Riker mount is a shallow cardboard box filled with cotton. Specimens are placed on the cotton and covered with a glass top.

Seal Riker mount with adhesive tape.

cotton batting
moth crystals

A cigar box makes a good insect box for a beginner.

CIGARS

Insect boxes with glass tops are available through biology supply houses.

BUTTERFLY COLLECTING

The finest-looking insect collection you can make is one that contains the most brilliant of our native butterflies and moths.

To make such a collection, you need some simple equipment, in addition to a net and killing jar—envelopes, spreading boards, and display boxes. And then, special insect pins and pinning forceps for proper handling of specimens.

JAPANESE BUTTERFLIES

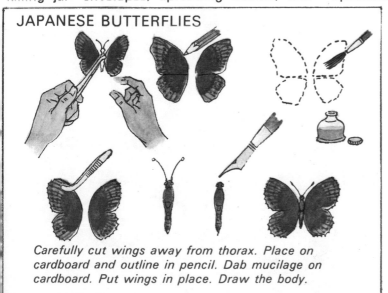

Carefully cut wings away from thorax. Place on cardboard and outline in pencil. Dab mucilage on cardboard. Put wings in place. Draw the body.

STYROFOAM MOUNT

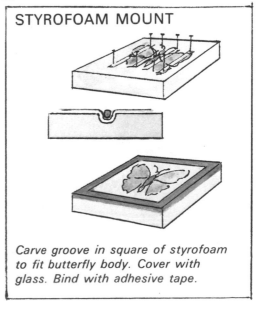

Carve groove in square of styrofoam to fit butterfly body. Cover with glass. Bind with adhesive tape.

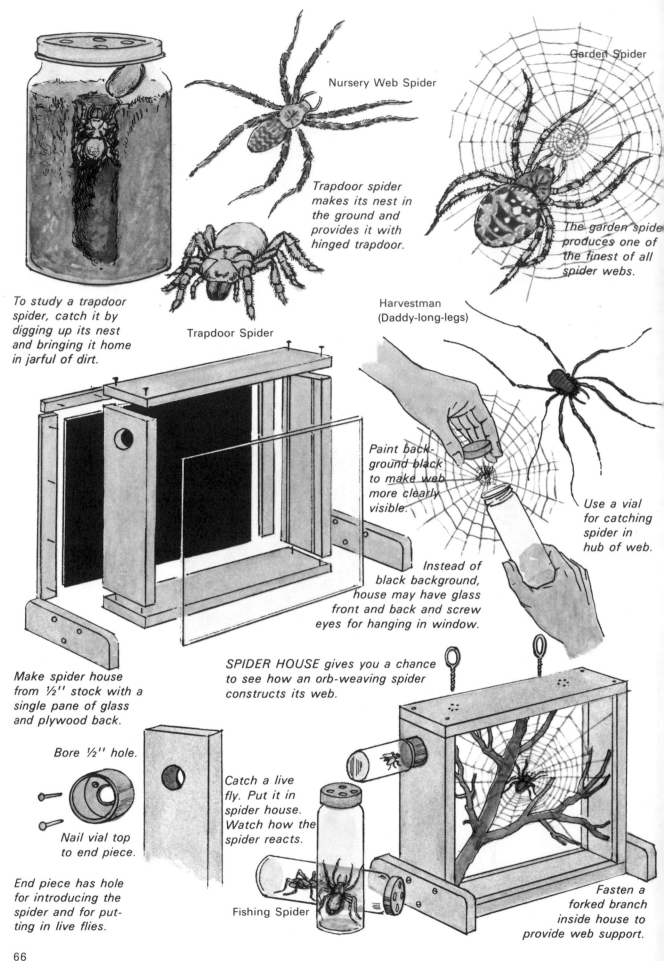

Nursery Web Spider

Garden Spider

Trapdoor spider makes its nest in the ground and provides it with hinged trapdoor.

The garden spider produces one of the finest of all spider webs.

To study a trapdoor spider, catch it by digging up its nest and bringing it home in jarful of dirt.

Trapdoor Spider

Harvestman (Daddy-long-legs)

Paint background black to make web more clearly visible.

Use a vial for catching spider in hub of web.

Instead of black background, house may have glass front and back and screw eyes for hanging in window.

Make spider house from ½'' stock with a single pane of glass and plywood back.

SPIDER HOUSE gives you a chance to see how an orb-weaving spider constructs its web.

Bore ½'' hole.

Nail vial top to end piece.

Catch a live fly. Put it in spider house. Watch how the spider reacts.

End piece has hole for introducing the spider and for putting in live flies.

Fishing Spider

Fasten a forked branch inside house to provide web support.

WATCHING FOR SPIDERS

To most people the two words ''spider'' and ''web'' belong together like ''ham'' and ''eggs.'' But the fact is that the majority of spiders do not make webs for snaring their prey. They get their food by hiding in flowers waiting to nab the insects that come for pollen or nectar, or by sneaking up on their victims and catching them by jumping on them or outrunning them.

Those that make webs are some of nature's most astonishing creatures. The web is made from threads that consist not of a single strand, but perhaps of a hundred strands. These strands issue, as a sticky fluid that immediately solidifies, from spinnerets at the tip of the spider's abdomen. Some spiders, such as the common house spider, make rather casual, tangled cobwebs in the corners of a room. Grass spiders make funnel-shaped nets among supporting blades of grass. Hammock spiders produce the flat horizontal webs which you may see when you look across a field in the early morning, when each strand is covered with dew.

The most spectacular of all spider webs are those made by the orb weavers, such as the golden garden spider. The construction of their vertical webs requires extraordinary engineering and architectural skills.

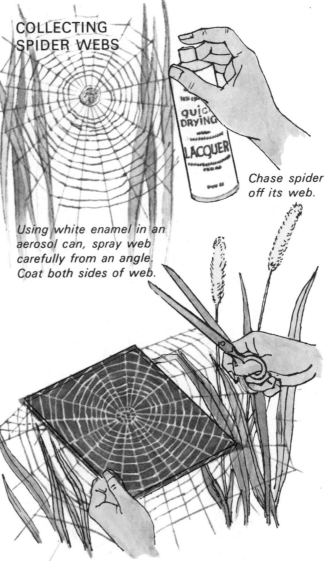

COLLECTING SPIDER WEBS

Chase spider off its web.

Using white enamel in an aerosol can, spray web carefully from an angle. Coat both sides of web.

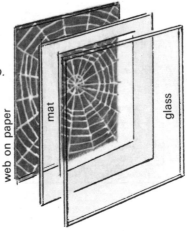

While still sticky, bring dark-colored construction paper in contact with web. Snip web loose with scissors.

Mount web under glass, with mat, if you like, between web and glass. Bind with tape.

web on paper   mat   glass

PHOTOGRAPHING SPIDER WEBS

Best web photos are shot in morning when dew is on web.

If no dew, produce your own from atomizer.

Study all angles. Best may be against sun. If so, shield the lens.

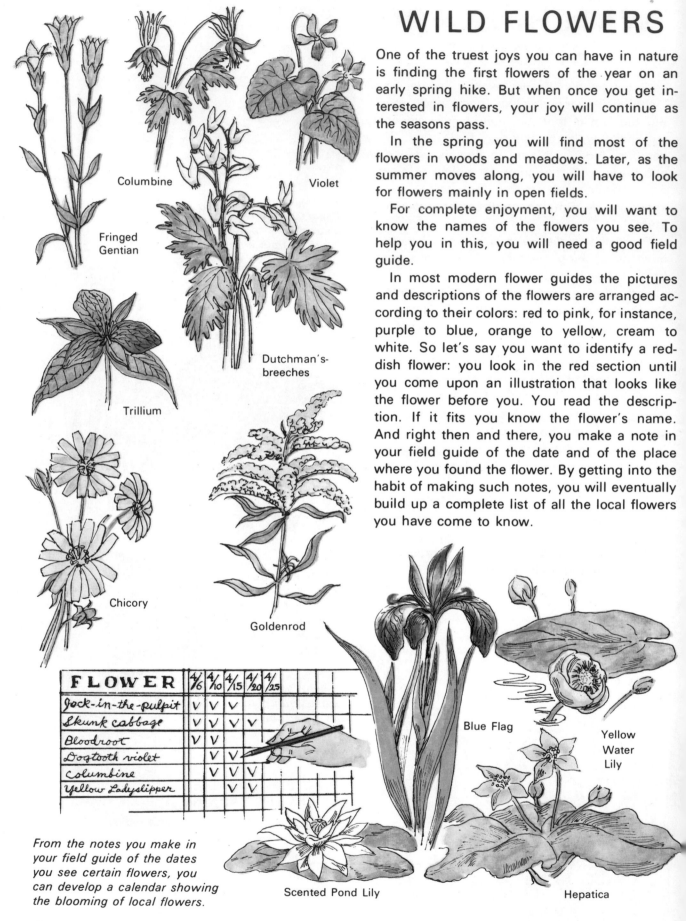

WILD FLOWERS

One of the truest joys you can have in nature is finding the first flowers of the year on an early spring hike. But when once you get interested in flowers, your joy will continue as the seasons pass.

In the spring you will find most of the flowers in woods and meadows. Later, as the summer moves along, you will have to look for flowers mainly in open fields.

For complete enjoyment, you will want to know the names of the flowers you see. To help you in this, you will need a good field guide.

In most modern flower guides the pictures and descriptions of the flowers are arranged according to their colors: red to pink, for instance, purple to blue, orange to yellow, cream to white. So let's say you want to identify a reddish flower: you look in the red section until you come upon an illustration that looks like the flower before you. You read the description. If it fits you know the flower's name. And right then and there, you make a note in your field guide of the date and of the place where you found the flower. By getting into the habit of making such notes, you will eventually build up a complete list of all the local flowers you have come to know.

Columbine

Fringed Gentian

Violet

Dutchman's-breeches

Trillium

Chicory

Goldenrod

Blue Flag

Yellow Water Lily

FLOWER	4/6	4/10	4/15	4/20	4/25
Jack-in-the-pulpit	V	V	V		
Skunk cabbage	V	V	V	V	
Bloodroot	V	V			
Dogtooth violet		V	V		
Columbine		V	V	V	
Yellow Ladyslipper			V	V	

From the notes you make in your field guide of the dates you see certain flowers, you can develop a calendar showing the blooming of local flowers.

Scented Pond Lily

Hepatica

Painted Cup

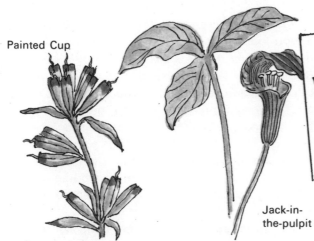

Jack-in-
the-pulpit

Yellow Lady-slipper

PROTECT OUR WILD FLOWERS

The best way to enjoy wild flowers is to study them right where they grow. And the best way to protect those that are rare is simply not to pluck them. Instead, take up flower photography.

If you want to have a wild flower corner in your home garden you can get some from nurseries that specialize in raising them.

Wild flowers you ordered from a nursery should be planted as soon as received. Learn from your field guide where the plants grow in nature and plant them in a spot as close to their natural conditions as possible.

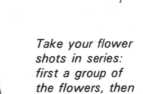

For especially pleasing flower photographs, focus sharply on the flower, then open up diaphragm to throw background out of focus for a soft effect.

Take your flower shots in series: first a group of the flowers, then a single flower.

A color shot of a single brilliant flower, thrown up to fill the screen, is a stunning sight.

DO NOT PICK WILD FLOWERS
SOME ARE PROTECTED BY LAW
HELP PROTECT NATURE

69

In digging up plants for your terrarium, be careful not to disturb the root system.

COLLECTING FOR TERRARIUMS

One of the most interesting features of nature is seeing things grow—in the plant world, seeing the seed develop into a tiny plant, watching the plant take on size and shape, following the formation of flowers and the setting of seeds. And then watching the whole process start all over.

It is easy enough to follow such development if you happen to live out in the country or if your family home is surrounded by a garden. But you can do it in the city as well by bringing living nature into your room at home. You and your family may already be enjoying a few ordinary house plants purchased from a local nursery or florist shop. But you will have more fun if you collect your own plants in the wild and take care of them yourself. The best way to do this is by establishing a terrarium.

Terrarium comes from the Latin word for earth, *terra,* and means, by dictionary definition, "a fully enclosed container for the indoor cultivation of plants." The two words "fully enclosed" are of great significance. They are the key to your success in raising wild plants indoors. The usual house plant, growing in its flower pot, needs perpetual care to prevent the soil from drying and the whole plant from wilting. By enclosing the plants, the moisture content of the plants and soil stays constant and you have no worry about taking care of the plants.

Your first attempt at creating a terrarium can be a very simple one. It will depend on the kind of "fully enclosed container" you can manage.

An old aquarium tank would be ideal, but would probably not be available. Next best would be a rectangular container, with a large cake pan for a base, four panes of glass for the walls, and yet another pane of glass for a cover—the panes held together with waterproof adhesive tape. Still another possibility would be using a box of clear plastic—or even creating

Depending on the kind of terrarium you plan to make, you will need some or all of this equipment: bags for soil and pebbles, plastic bags and small containers for plants, trowel, hand spade.

a small indoor garden in a cake pan and completely enclosing it in a plastic bag. By looking around to see what is available, you may be able to come up with an idea of your own for a terrarium case.

Having established the size of your terrarium, the important job now comes of filling it. For this you need enough small pebbles to make a 1'' layer for drainage, enough good soil for a 2'' layer, and plants of suitable size. So, off you go on a terrarium hike, bringing with you a few plastic bags, a number of small containers, and the tools for digging up plants.

The selection of plants depends on your own taste and on the time of the year. In the early spring you will find many flat leaf rosettes that will turn into flowering plants, and seedlings of different trees. In the fall, you will look for low, creeping plants. Throughout the year, mosses and small ferns may be your choice. Dig up the plants with some dirt adhering to the roots, and plant them as soon as you get home.

An old aquarium tank—even a leaky one—will make a good terrarium case. It will require a glass or plastic cover.

You can make a terrarium case from a cake pan and 4 panes of glass plus a cover.

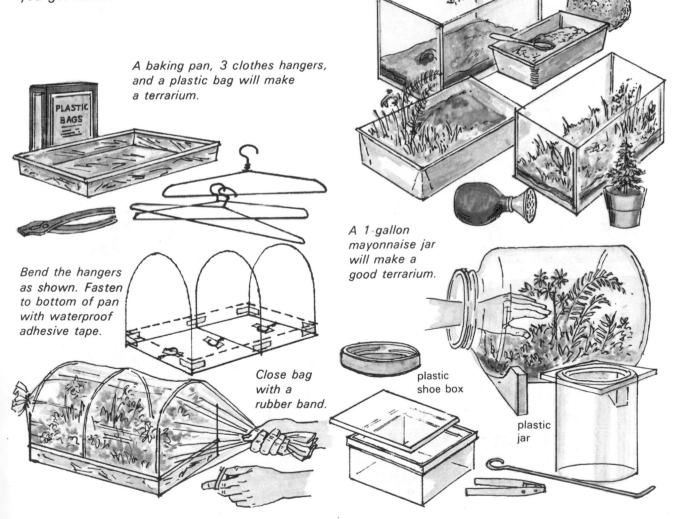

A baking pan, 3 clothes hangers, and a plastic bag will make a terrarium.

PLASTIC BAGS

Bend the hangers as shown. Fasten to bottom of pan with waterproof adhesive tape.

Close bag with a rubber band.

A 1-gallon mayonnaise jar will make a good terrarium.

plastic shoe box

plastic jar

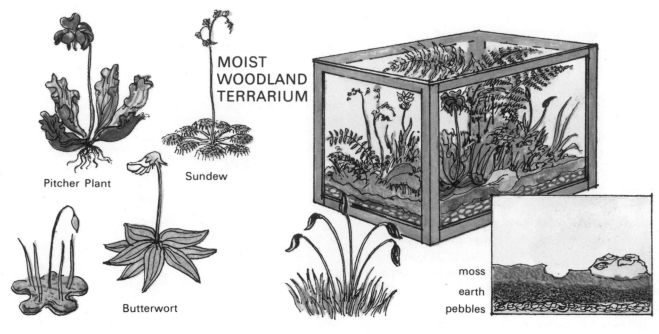

Pitcher Plant

Sundew

MOIST WOODLAND TERRARIUM

Butterwort

Liverwort

Moss

moss
earth
pebbles

MAKING TERRARIUMS

After you have established a terrarium along general lines, you may want to specialize in developing a terrarium of a specific environmental type or for a specific purpose.

The two most popular environmental terrariums are the moist woodland terrarium and the desert terrarium. A sod terrarium provides for hours of intensive study. A decorative terrarium will add color to your home. For each of the first three, it pays to buy a regular terrarium case or aquarium tank from your local department store or hobby shop. Pick one of a

suitable size for the space you have available. For the decorative terrarium, any clear glass container will do.

To make up a moist woodland terrarium, you begin by spreading a 1″ layer of pebbles on the bottom of your case. This is followed by a 2″ layer of leaf mold. Then plant a few small ferns, some low, flowering woodland plants, and, perhaps, a couple of evergreen seedlings. If possible, introduce one or two of the insect-eating bog plants that help make this kind of terrarium especially interesting: sun-

DESERT TERRARIUM

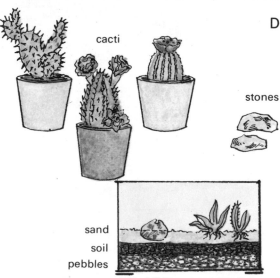

cacti

stones

sand
soil
pebbles

Put in layers of pebbles, soil, and sand. Plant with cacti and succulent plants.

Use glass plate only to keep climbing lizards within case.

Desert terrarium needs very little care. Drip water at roots of each cactus every week or so.

SOD TERRARIUM

Water generously.

Cut a 3''-thick piece of sod to fit your terrarium.

Place sod in terrarium case on top of layer of pebbles.

Cover with glass plate.

Watch developments. Make lists of plant and animal life.

dew, pitcher plant, butterwort. If you haven't found any of these plants on your hikes, you will be able to secure them from a biological supply house. Finish by placing clumps of moss or lichens among the other plants. Sprinkle your production with water and cover with a glass plate. Your woodland terrarium will be of even greater interest if you inhabit it with a couple of live newts or salamanders.

Begin the desert terrarium by pouring in first a layer of pebbles, then a layer of garden soil and another of sand. Plant different kinds of small cacti, a few tufts of low grass, and a couple of succulent plants. Add small stones or remains of desert plants for decoration. Here again, you may want to add some animal life, such as a lizard or a small snake.

A sod terrarium also starts with pouring in a layer of pebbles. The next step is to measure the length and width of the terrarium case and to cut a 3''-thick piece of sod to fit it snugly. Water the sod and cover the terrarium with a glass plate. Watch the developments from day to day. You will be surprised. The grass will grow and weeds you did not know were in the soil will shoot up. But besides, you will be amazed at the animal life in your terrarium: earthworms aerating the soil, grubs turning into beetles, ants scurrying about.

There is no limit to the kind of decorative terrarium you can make. It depends on what glass container you have available. You can use anything from a globular fish bowl to a brandy snifter.

DECORATIVE TERRARIUM

Scoop holes for plants, using a small spoon.

Use a piece of decorative glassware.

Put in layers of pebbles and soil.

Insert plants by hand or with the help of wooden tweezers.

YOUR BOTANICAL COLLECTION

As you get deeper into the study of wild flowers, you will learn that botanists, over the years, have arranged the flowers of the world into different families. Each plant family has its own characteristics. In a flower belonging to the rose family, for instance, the main parts that make up the flower—the petals and sepals—are divisible by 5, in the mustard family by 4, in the lily family by 3. What looks like a single flower of the composite family may actually be hundreds of flowers, some of them tube shaped, others tongue shaped. Members of the pea family are recognized by their typical pea flowers, of the figwort family by their fancy, irregular flowers.

For the closer study that is necessary for knowing the flowers by their families, you may want to establish a botanical collection—a herbarium—of your own.

Keeping well away from collecting rare and protected wild flowers, you will quickly discover that there are thousands of others that grow in such profusion that there is no chance

When collecting flower specimens, either place them in a field press on the spot, or bring the plants home in cornucopias rolled from newspapers and keep in a plastic bag to prevent wilting.

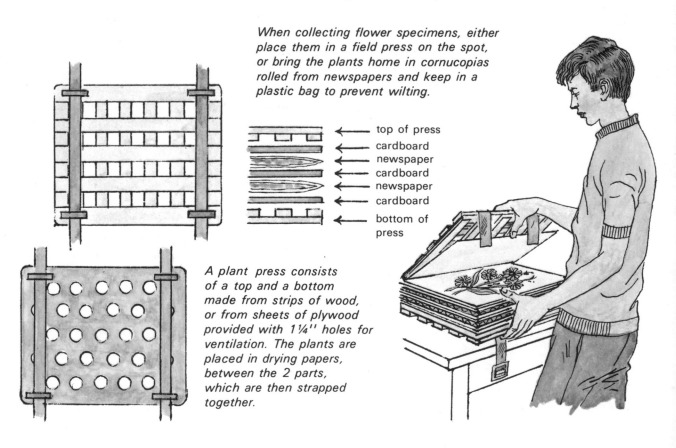

← top of press
← cardboard
← newspaper
← cardboard
← newspaper
← cardboard
← bottom of press

A plant press consists of a top and a bottom made from strips of wood, or from sheets of plywood provided with 1¼'' holes for ventilation. The plants are placed in drying papers, between the 2 parts, which are then strapped together.

ever of eradicating them. That goes especially for all those plants we refer to as "weeds."

In collecting botanical specimens be sure that you get all parts of the plant: flowers, stems, leaves, roots. Then, after collecting, either put the specimens into a field press right then and there, or bring them home, properly protected, and arrange them for pressing at home.

The pressing of plants is done by putting them between sheets of newspapers or blotters and placing them for drying in a special plant press or under a stack of heavy books. After a few days, change the papers and continue pressing until the plants have dried. To speed the drying, you may want to insert pieces of corrugated cardboard among the plants.

When completely dry, place each pressed specimen on a sheet of thin, white cardboard and hold it in position with tiny strips of gummed paper or self-adhesive sealing tape. Label each sheet with correct information about the plant, giving its name, place where found, and date when found. Keep the mounted plants in folders, with a folder for each plant family.

When completely dry, place specimens on sheets of cardboard and hold in place with strips of tape.

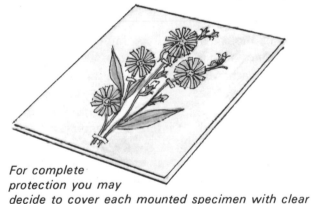

For complete protection you may decide to cover each mounted specimen with clear plastic food wrap.

WINTER BOUQUETS

Certain weed stalks make spectacular, everlasting winter bouquets: cattail, mullein, milkweed, wild carrot, yarrow, goldenrod. Hang them up to dry, protected by a paper bag.

For long-term keeping or for special effect spray bouquet with fixative or enamel.

MARINE SPECIMENS

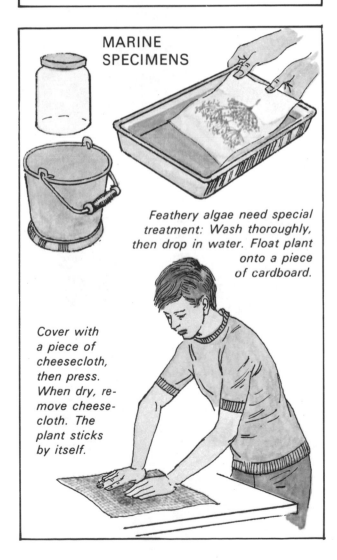

Feathery algae need special treatment: Wash thoroughly, then drop in water. Float plant onto a piece of cardboard.

Cover with a piece of cheesecloth, then press. When dry, remove cheesecloth. The plant sticks by itself.

TREES

Among all living things, trees are about the easiest to get to know. They are large so you can't possibly miss seeing them. They stay put, thus giving you a chance to study them thoroughly. They have distinguishing marks that make it fairly easy to tell them apart.

We have more than 600 native trees in the United States. But don't let that number worry you as you set out to learn to recognize trees and call them by their names. You will quickly realize that since some trees like it hot, others cool, some like to have their roots in loose, dry soil, others in rich, moist soil. They won't all be growing in your neighborhood, not even in your state. So simply go to work learning to know the trees in your immediate vicinity. You will then discover that if you can recognize a couple of dozen trees, you'll know practically all the trees you are apt to come upon on your hikes.

To help you in this, keep in mind that trees are generally grouped into two large groups. The first of these groups comprises the conifers—meaning the cone bearers. These trees have needlelike or scalelike leaves that usually stay on the trees for several years, creating an "evergreen" effect. In this group we have the pine, hemlock, fir, spruce, larch, and cedar. The other large group includes the so-called broad-leaved trees—all of them with more or less broad, flat leaves. The broad-leaved trees are also called deciduous trees—from a Latin word that means "to fall"—because in cold climates they shed their leaves in the autumn, with the result that the trees look naked throughout the winter. In this group we have the willows and poplars, the birches and oaks, the maples and ashes, and many others. The conifers are the commonest trees in the West, the broad-leaved in the East. In addition to these two large groups, we have a small group of about a dozen different trees: the palms, all of them growing in the warmer regions of the South.

Some trees you will quickly be able to recognize by their shape, even from a distance: the cone-shaped spruces and firs, the vase-shaped elms, the broad-sweeping oaks. Their bark gives away some of the trees: the shaggy bark of the shagbark hickory, the blotched

The shape of many trees will tell you their family.

For complete identification, check such details as bark, leaf, flower, fruit.

bark of sycamore, the smooth gray of beech, the blond curls of yellow birch, the chalky-white bark of gray birch. There's no mistaking the leaves of the tulip tree that look as if their tips were snipped off, the four kinds of leaves on the same sassafras tree, the spiny leaves of the holly. And you will have no trouble recognizing dogwood and magnolia, locust and redbud by their beautiful flowers. Still other trees you can tell by their seeds or fruits—the pines and spruces by their cones, the oaks by their acorns, the maples by their keys, the wild cherries, haws, persimmons and pawpaws by their fleshy fruits.

If you combine interest in trees with a certain amount of drawing ability, you can make yourself a spectacular series of tree "portraits" by sketching on large sheets the details of individual trees: general shape, shape of leaf, flower, fruit. Or you can concentrate on leaves in all their various forms: feather veined or hand veined, smooth edged or sawtooth edged, lobed or notched, or cut into several leaflets.

Even an ordinary snapshot camera will make it possible for you to take detail shots of all the parts of a tree, as well as a series of silhouettes of the same tree throughout the seasons of the year, showing it in bud, in full leaf, in fall foliage, and completely stripped of its leaves in winter. And then, for a special treat, you may go on a color slide expedition some autumn to catch the brilliant red of staghorn sumac, the scarlet of sugar maple, the orange of sassafras, the bright yellow of aspen and birch, and the in-between colors of many other trees.

Start tree photography any time of the year.

Even a snapshot camera is good for tree shots.

If you like to sketch, a tree gives you many chances to test your ability.

Porcupines use tree limbs for rest places on their travels, and damage the trees by gnawing off the bark.

A beaver can cut down a tree in a few minutes with its powerful teeth.

Bears often claw and rub themselves against certain trees.

Moose and other members of the deer family may browse all the lower branches off a tree. A moose may also bend down a sapling to the ground by straddling it, to browse on its upper branches.

BE A TREE DETECTIVE

Instead of trying to learn a little about a great number of trees you may get a special thrill out of finding out a great number of things about one single tree. For this purpose you pick a tree that seems to have special possibilities and turn yourself into a tree detective.

Just the way a regular detective trying to track down a person begins by asking, "What does he look like? What's his name? Where

Hard shells of larger nuts do not stop a squirrel from getting kernel.

Nuts with tiny teeth marks show presence of mice.

does he live? With whom does he associate?" you can go about your tree-detecting in the same fashion.

"What does the tree look like?" What shape has it? How tall is it, how wide is its crown? How thick is the trunk? How old would it be, approximately? Is the trunk straight or bent, single or divided? Is the bark rough or smooth? What is the shape of the leaves? Does the tree have any flowers, any fruits?

"What's its name?" With the questions above answered, you should have no trouble finding its name in your tree guide.

"Where does it live?" Where is its actual location on the map of the area? Does the tree stand in the middle of a forest, at the forest edge, all alone out in the open? What soil does it live in—poor or rich, dry or moist?

"With whom does it associate?" A detective might visit all the floors of an apartment house to check on associates of the person he is tracing. In the same way, you may want to seek information about the animal life that has had some association with your tree. So, think of the tree, for a moment, as a tall apartment house, and start investigating. What creatures, beneficial or harmful (earthworms, grubs, beetles), live in the subbasement? Any small animals, such as mice or chipmunks, in the basement (among the roots)? Did the tree have any animal guests that left their "visiting cards"—scratches of claws, tearing off of bark, gnawing into the wood? Have any animals moved into the cavities in the upper stories? What birds live in the topmost floors? As you discover the answers by actual investigation, write up a short report of your findings.

So much for a living tree. But you may also be interested in doing your detective work on a tree stump you come upon. This takes another set of questions.

How old was the tree when it was cut down? (The annual rings will tell the story.) Why was it cut down? (Perhaps the fire scar had something to do with that.) During what years of its life did the tree have its slowest growth, its fastest growth? (Again, the annual rings will provide you with information.) Did the insects invade the tree early in its life or after it was damaged by the fire? (Determine by the number of annual rings penetrated.)

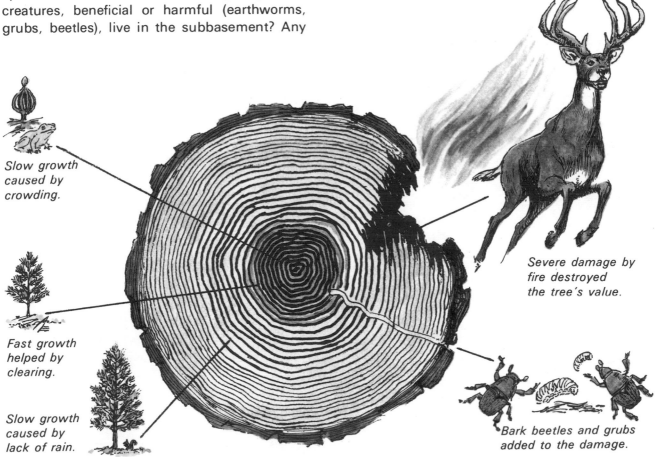

Slow growth caused by crowding.

Fast growth helped by clearing.

Slow growth caused by lack of rain.

Severe damage by fire destroyed the tree's value.

Bark beetles and grubs added to the damage.

CARBON PAPER PRINTS

The simplest and least messy method of making leaf prints is to use ordinary carbon paper. Place the leaf on a smooth surface, with the veiny side up. Place a piece of carbon paper on top of the leaf, with the carbon side up.

Cover carbon paper with a piece of white paper. Hold everything firmly in place. Rub on top of the white paper with the back of a teaspoon.

Rubbing transfers carbon to underside of white paper.

LEAF PRINTING

Leaf printing is a popular hobby among people interested in trees. The methods for producing leaf prints are simple ones and the results can be very pleasing and gratifying. You can use freshly-picked leaves for leaf printing, but dried leaves are better for the purpose.

One easy method consists of spattering the outline of the leaf onto a piece of construction paper with drops of ink or enamel. This method makes a silhouette of the leaf—white or colored depending on the color of the paper.

Another method uses the leaf as a printing block to produce a print that will show all the veins of the leaf. Here again, by using different colored linoleum-block printing inks, you can develop an interesting series of prints for your scrapbook of all the trees you know.

SPATTER PRINTS

In a spatter print, you get a blank leaf outlined by thousands of tiny enamel or ink drops.

For quickest way of making spatter print, pin paper onto large piece of cardboard. Outline leaf with the fine spray from an aerosol spray can of enamel.

Another method is to use construction paper and ink. Place leaf on sheet of paper. Dip toothbrush lightly in ink. Point toothbrush toward leaf. Rub a nail or knife over the bristles toward you.

In snapping back, the bristles spatter tiny ink drops onto the paper. Outline whole leaf in this way. Then let print dry.

PRINTING-INK PRINTS

Get a tube of printing ink for linoleum blocks from an art store. With rubber roller, spread a small amount evenly onto a glass plate.

Ink veiny side of leaf. Place leaf, inked side down, on white paper. Cover with newspaper. Use roller to press leaf against printing paper.

NOTE: In making spatter prints, protect surrounding areas against spray with newspaper.

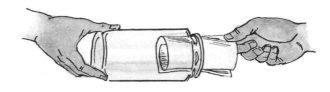

You can actually photograph leaves without a camera by using dry-print paper procurable from store selling materials for architects.

PHOTO PRINTS OF LEAVES

Make printing frame by taping glass plate to plywood. In subdued light, place dry-print paper on the plywood, then leaf on paper. Close frame. Expose to full sunlight until yellow color has turned white.

To develop print, slip paper into a glass jar. Place jar down over tiny cup filled with household ammonia. Print develops within a few seconds.

LEAF COLLECTIONS

When studying trees you will become intrigued by the great variety you will find in the shapes of their leaves.

Some tree leaves are narrow, such as the willows; others are broad, such as the magnolias. Some have smooth edges (black gum and dogwood, for instance), others have sawtoothed edges (elm and birch), still others are lobed (sassafras and many of the oaks). Some leaves are heart shaped (redbud and basswood), others hand shaped (the maples). The leaves of hickories and ashes and locust are split up in a number of leaflets.

In collecting tree leaves, pick a few leaves that are completely typical from each tree. Select only those that are perfect, without insect holes or other blemishes. Press them by the same method used in pressing flowers (page 75). When completely dry, mount one specimen of each tree on a sheet of thin cardboard by one of the methods shown below. Use extra leaves for making leaf prints.

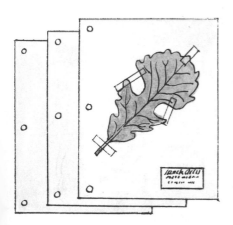

Dried leaves may be mounted onto loose-leaf sheets with tape, or glued to the sheets with thin layer of mucilage.

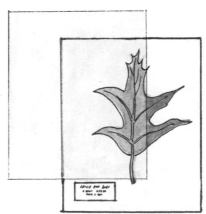

For special protection, you may want to cover each of your leaf mounts with sheet of clear plastic.

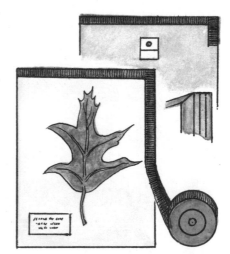

For wall decoration, cover leaf mount with glass, bind with adhesive tape.

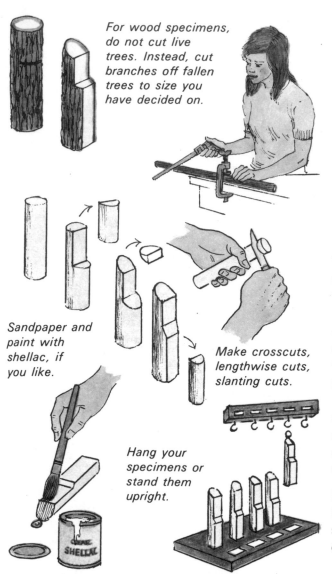

For wood specimens, do not cut live trees. Instead, cut branches off fallen trees to size you have decided on.

Sandpaper and paint with shellac, if you like.

Make crosscuts, lengthwise cuts, slanting cuts.

Hang your specimens or stand them upright.

OTHER TREE COLLECTIONS

To collect leaves, you have to wait until early summer to secure the best specimens. But there are other collections connected with trees that you can make at other times. The collecting of various woods and different types of bark can be undertaken any time of the year. The seasons for collecting buds are late winter and very early spring; for collecting tree seeds, the fall of the year.

WOOD COLLECTIONS A collection of wood specimens gives you a chance to study the interior structure of a tree. It will make you marvel at the fact that millions of cells can grow together to form a substance as soft and as easily carved as white pine or as hard as the maple wood used for making fine furniture.

In making your collection, settle on a reasonable length and thickness for your specimens. Then cut them with various cuts—crosswise, lengthwise, slanting—to show all the features of the wood.

BARK COLLECTIONS Each kind of tree has its own special kind of bark. Some trees have smooth bark that fits tightly around the trunks, others have rough bark that flakes off as the

For bark rubbings, ring the tree with shelf paper or some other kind of soft paper.

Make rubbings with crayon or, far better, shoemaker's burnishing wax. Trim finished rubbings down to the size you want for your collection.

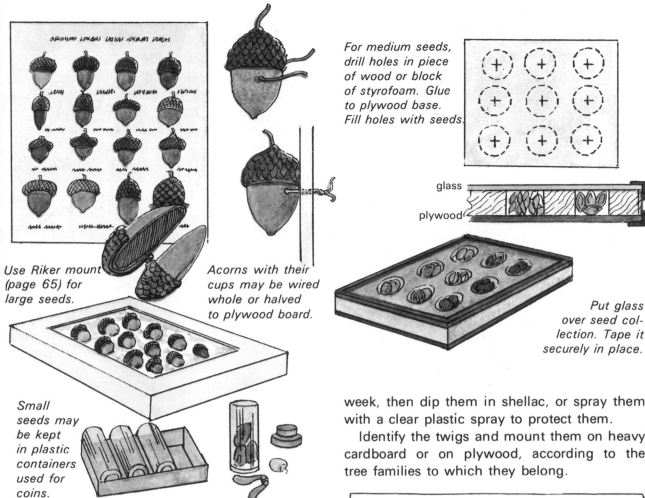

Use Riker mount (page 65) for large seeds.

Acorns with their cups may be wired whole or halved to plywood board.

Small seeds may be kept in plastic containers used for coins.

For medium seeds, drill holes in piece of wood or block of styrofoam. Glue to plywood base. Fill holes with seeds.

glass

plywood

Put glass over seed collection. Tape it securely in place.

trees grow older, still others have coarse and deeply furrowed bark.

The best way of studying and comparing different kinds of bark is with the help of a collection of bark rubbings. Such rubbings will also help in identifying trees, in the same way that fingerprints are used for identifying people.

TREE SEED COLLECTIONS Tree seeds are collected when completely ripe and dry—in other words, when they start falling off the trees.

For identification, be sure to include the cups of acorns, the shells of hickory nuts, the pods of black locust and redbud, as well as similar features of other trees.

TWIG AND BUD COLLECTIONS For a twig and bud collection, decide on the length you want the twigs to be, then cut them to this length with slanting cuts. Let them dry for a

week, then dip them in shellac, or spray them with a clear plastic spray to protect them.

Identify the twigs and mount them on heavy cardboard or on plywood, according to the tree families to which they belong.

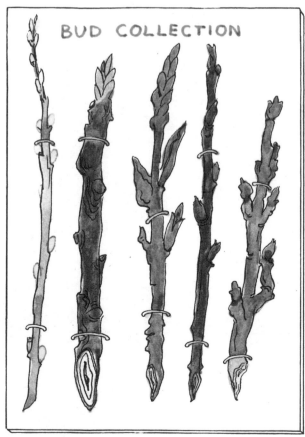

BUD COLLECTION

GROWING TREES

"A man does not plant a tree for himself," said a poet once, "he plants it for posterity." By planting a tree, you secure for yourself a bit of immortality: the tree will probably be continuing its growth long after you have passed out of the picture—provided you planted the right kind of tree in the right kind of soil.

Why plant a tree? There are lots of reasons. If your home has a garden, you may want to plant certain trees to add to the beauty of your home, or to provide shade, or for their fruits. Planting trees on your school grounds or in Boy Scout or Girl Scout camp may be for the same reasons, but also for assuring added opportunities for outdoor living. Commercial lumber and paper companies plant trees by the score for each tree they cut down, in order to have a sustained yield of timber for all kinds of building construction and pulp for the making of paper and numerous other products. In state and national parks, new trees are planted perpetually to replace old trees that may have been destroyed by insect pests or in forest fires. Here it is not only a matter of perpetuating recreational facilities for hikers and campers, but also of guaranteeing food and shelter and living space for wildlife, and of controlling the flow of streams by protecting the watershed.

There is a very special satisfaction to planting a few trees and following their growth over the years.

In transplanting trees, the main consideration is the protection of the roots.

Nursery stock, grown in pots, is more easily transplanted than wildlings.

Larger trees for transplanting are dug up with a ball of dirt which is protected by burlap.

After planting or transplanting, water thoroughly to establish the tree firmly and keep it growing.

84

Equipment for planting seedlings: mattock or dibble bar, pail with water.

In planting seedlings with a mattock, drive mattock straight into the ground. Raise handle to produce hole. Plant the seedling. Drive mattock down and push soil toward plant. Firm the ground with foot.

In planting with a dibble bar, drive bar slantingly into ground, then raise to form hole. Place seedling. Insert bar again. Pull back to firm soil at bottom of roots, then push forward to firm soil at top of roots.

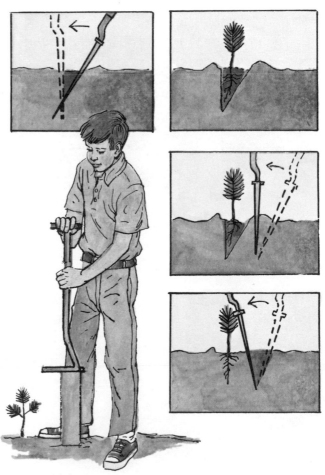

Putting trees around your home is not so much a matter of planting as it is of transplanting—moving trees already established from the wilds or from a tree nursery to your own garden. If you can get permission from a forester to dig up a wildling for transplanting, it makes a lot of difference if the tree is an evergreen or a deciduous tree. Evergreens have a shallow root system that is quite easily dug up and replanted. Deciduous trees, on the other hand, have a taproot that extends far into the ground and therefore need extreme care in moving and resetting. In most cases, you will be better off if you purchase the trees for your home grounds from a tree nursery. The best time for planting them is the fall, after the sap has stopped flowing.

For a large-scale planting of trees, such as for school grounds or camp, you will probably be working with your school friends or Scout pals, putting in seedlings, perhaps by the hundreds, instead of transplanting a few large trees. Such seedlings—preferably two- or three-year-old conifer seedlings or one-year-old deciduous tree seedlings—may be secured from a local nursery. The forestry services of many of our states make such seedlings available free or at low cost.

Obsidian

Feldspar

Volcanic Bomb

Basalt

Scoria

Pumice

IGNEOUS ROCKS From the very name (ignis is Latin for fire) you will know that these rocks were created at high temperatures, under very great pressure.

Sandstone

Sandy Sha

Conglomera

SEDIMENTARY ROCKS were formed by sediment: small particles that built up layer upon layer. The upper layers squeezed the lower layers into solid rocks

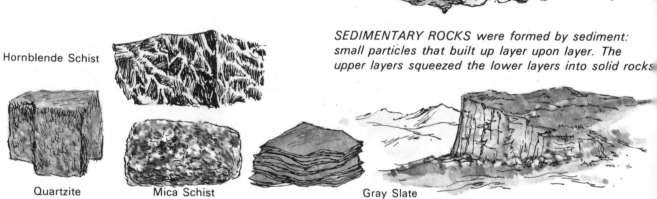

Hornblende Schist

Quartzite

Mica Schist

Gray Slate

METAMORPHIC ROCKS are igneous and sedimentary rocks which, under heat, pressure, and other great influences, have changed into something else.

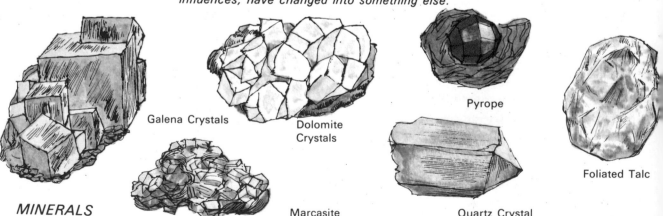

Galena Crystals

Dolomite Crystals

Pyrope

Foliated Talc

MINERALS

Marcasite

Quartz Crystal

ROCKS, MINERALS AND FOSSILS

When you deal with rocks and minerals—the chemicals that make up the rocks—you deal with the oldest things on earth, the very ingredients that make up its crust. As a matter of fact, some of the rocks you pick up on a hike may have been formed comparatively soon after the birth of the earth. This might make them 4½ billion years old or older, according to recent estimates.

Using methods invented within the last few years, scientists have become able to figure out the approximate age of certain rock formations. They can also calculate when certain upheavals took place that changed the features of the landscape. And they can determine, from fossils, during which geological ages life came to earth—when the first plant life began and when the earliest forms of animals made their appearance, millions of years ago.

So when you take up the study of rocks (petrology) or of minerals (mineralogy) or of fossils (paleontology), you are delving into the past as far back as human knowledge and imagination can take you.

Because of the upheaval of the ground, you may find fossils even on a mountain ridge.

The fossils of shells will tell you that the place was once the bottom of the sea.

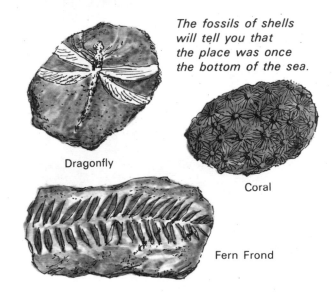

Dragonfly

Coral

Fern Frond

FOSSILS are the actual remains or the changed remains or the imprints of dead plants or animal life. They are always found in sedimentary rocks—never in igneous or metamorphic rocks. Some fossils may be the actual shells of sea animals. Some were formed by replacement—such as petrified wood, where the walls of the cells were replaced with agate.

The fossilized imprints of ancient plants and animal life may be found in such sedimentary rocks as shale and limestone.

Fossilized tracks of dinosaurs were formed when the animals made imprints in mud which hardened and were later filled with other matter.

FINDING ROCKS AND MINERALS

Wherever you go on a nature hike, there will be rocks right under your feet.

In the mountainous parts of our country— the Rockies in the West, the Appalachian range in the East, the states of New England, the Pacific coast—you may actually be climbing over the exposed surfaces of the original igneous or metamorphic rocks of these areas.

In some of the states to the north, the rocks and boulders you encounter may not be natives at all—they may have been carried down from the North about 2 million years ago, during the Ice Age, when vast masses of ice spread down over our continent.

In the Midwest and the South, sedimentary bedrock of sandstone or limestone may be several feet below the surface, but the soil you step on will be rock nevertheless, ground into powder by wind and water and turned into a complex mixture by the addition of decayed vegetable and animal matter.

If you live among mountains, you'll have no trouble finding rocks and minerals. But whether your neighborhood is truly mountainous or not, look for specimens first of all where they may be naturally exposed in your locality: in outcrops, in cliffs and ridges, along the seacoast, in valleys where rivers have eroded deep gashes into the banks. Even an old, dried-up stream bed may contain gravel and pebbles and rocks that may prove of interest—after all, it was in just such a location that gold was first discovered in California. Although your Southwestern deserts may seem unlikely places for rock collecting, they are avidly searched by thousands of "rock hounds" for special rocks, for petrified wood, and for a great variety of minerals that may be lying loose on the desert sand as "floats," or that may be imbedded in some outcrop.

Next to natural locations, look for places where rocks and minerals may be exposed through the work of people, such as where excavations are being made for the construction of some large building, where hills are being bulldozed for the making of a new highway, where the foundations are being prepared for a new bridge.

Deserts may have outcrops of rocks and may offer minerals as "floats."

A stream may be full of interesting rocks eroded out of the banks.

Sandstone cliffs are often carved into weird shapes by wind erosion.

A quarry gives you a chance to find rocks and to study rock formations.

Here's the equipment for a geological field trip. You'll also need tough clothing and sturdy shoes.

If yours is a mining area, you may be able to get permission to search through the waste dumpings for rocks and minerals. And if you can locate a stone quarry nearby, the owner may let you rummage through some of the rock rubble or even let you study the quarry face itself in a nonworking part of the quarry.

The day you decide to take up rock and mineral collecting in earnest, you will need a few pieces of equipment.

The most important is a good geological hammer. Such hammers come with two different kinds of heads: one has a chisel head and is intended for ''soft'' (sedimentary) rocks; the other has a pick head for use on ''hard'' (igneous and metamorphic) rocks. The most important uses for a geological hammer are to expose a weathered rock surface to find out what the rock really looks like; to break off specimens; to lay open certain rounded rocks that may look like lumps of clay, but are actually ''geodes'' that may be hollow inside and lined with numerous mineral crystals. In addition to the hammer, you will probably want one or two chisels for extra-careful work in removing samples and for digging minerals out of their rock bases.

For safety's sake, when working with hammers and chisels always keep your eyes protected with a pair of goggles. You may also want to protect your hands by wearing cotton work gloves.

In addition to these pieces of equipment, you need wrapping materials to prevent your specimens from being damaged by rubbing against each other—newspaper will do—and a sturdy knapsack for carrying home your loot. Field book, notebook, and pencils require no explanation. Neither do map and compass if you expect your rock-collecting expedition to take you far up into the mountains.

Protect each rock specimen by wrapping it in paper.

Roll up specimen.   Fold over ends of paper.

ROCK AND MINERAL COLLECTIONS

Do you remember the days when you used to come back from a hike with the pockets of your jeans weighted down with pebbles and stones you had decided to bring home because they looked so "pretty" or had intrigued you by their shape? You won't get far with that kind of collection. For a rock collection to be good, it should tell a story.

This may be a comparatively simple story of the geological history of your county or state, told by means of representative specimens correctly identified, and by a map with the places where found clearly marked. Or it may be a personal story of your geological travels at home and abroad, with photographs of the mountains or cliffs, seacoasts or canyons, where you found the specimens. Or it may be a scientific story of just one type of rock: sedimentary, igneous, metamorphic.

For telling any one of these stories, you may decide to leave the rocks the way they are.

When trimming rocks, protect your eyes with goggles.

For a neat rock collection, trim all specimens to a uniform size, such as 1" by 1½" or 2" by 3".

If specimen has prominent mineral crystals, do not knock them off in trimming.

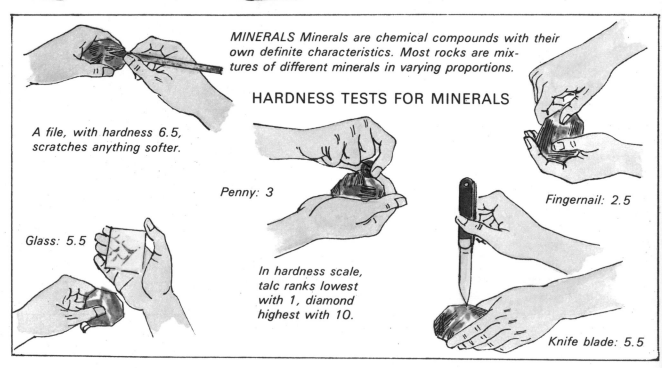

MINERALS Minerals are chemical compounds with their own definite characteristics. Most rocks are mixtures of different minerals in varying proportions.

HARDNESS TESTS FOR MINERALS

A file, with hardness 6.5, scratches anything softer.

Penny: 3

Fingernail: 2.5

Glass: 5.5

In hardness scale, talc ranks lowest with 1, diamond highest with 10.

Knife blade: 5.5

Wash your rock specimens and clean them with a stiff brush. Then dry.

Write labels in India ink, giving identification and place where found.

Or you may want to trim them down, as most collectors do, to a uniform size: 1″ by 1½″ if you want them real small, 2″ by 3″ if you want them larger. When trimmed to the same size, you have a better means of comparing their structure and of making a finer display of them as you arrange them in the partitioned trays you have made for your shelves or your drawers.

An egg box is a good temporary container when starting a mineral collection.

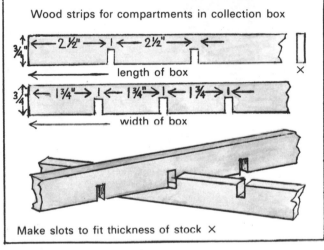

Wood strips for compartments in collection box

length of box

width of box

Make slots to fit thickness of stock ✕

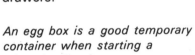

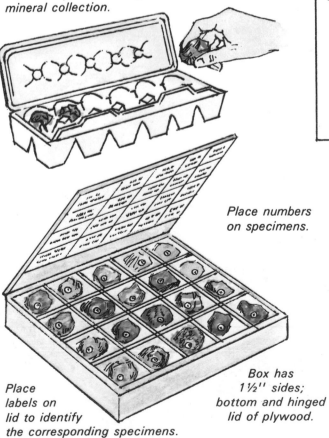

Place numbers on specimens.

Place labels on lid to identify the corresponding specimens.

Box has 1½″ sides; bottom and hinged lid of plywood.

Spectacular minerals may be mounted or enclosed in glass.

LAPIDARY

A great number of young rock collectors graduate, by easy stages, from ''pebble pups'' through ''rock hounds'' into lapidarians—practitioners of the ancient art of lapidary, the cutting and polishing of precious and semi-precious stones.

The first step along the way is rock tumbling. This consists of tumbling small rocks in a homemade or commercial tumbling barrel, made to revolve at a certain speed 24 hours a day. When this tumbling is done in the presence of water and different grades of silicon carbide, the rocks are smoothed down into various pleasing shapes, often of great beauty. The stones are then polished. You may include them in your collection or turn them into pendants for bracelets or necklaces.

The next step in becoming an expert lapidarian involves actual gem cutting. You will probably never have a chance to cut a diamond, but you may satisfy yourself by turning pieces of rock into cabochons—gems that have a smooth, convex surface. Any rock or mineral harder than 4 on the hardness scale can be made into a cabochon. The most popular stones for the purpose are agates, jasper, and petrified wood. For cutting cabochons, you need a commercial cutter and grinder. You may get this in a local hobby or mineral shop.

For rock tumbling, pick specimens as small in diameter as a dime, as large as a quarter.

Unless rocks are pleasantly formed by nature, you may pre-form them with chisel and hammer.

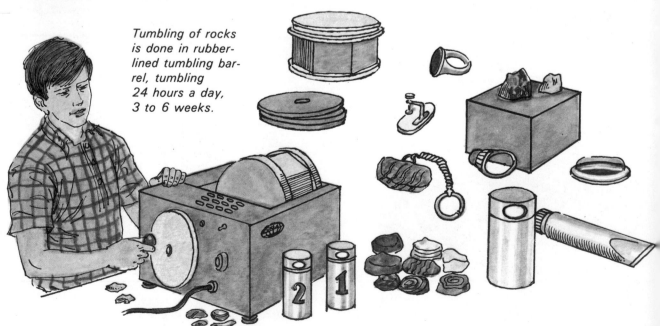

Tumbling of rocks is done in rubber-lined tumbling barrel, tumbling 24 hours a day, 3 to 6 weeks.

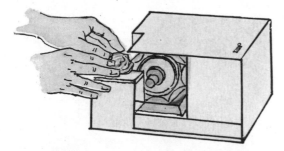

The first step in making a cabochon is to cut a ½" slice off a suitable rock with a diamond saw.

1

When sawing, hold the rock with both hands.

2

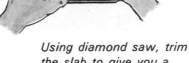

Using template, trace shape desired onto slab with help of an aluminum nail.

Using diamond saw, trim the slab to give you a piece of size you want.

3

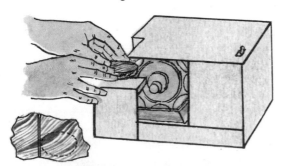

Commercial gem maker comes with diamond saw blade, grinding wheel, sanding and polishing discs.

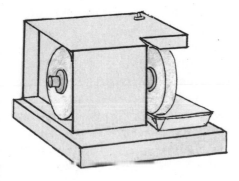

When ground to proper shape and size, the stone is sanded on two grades of silicon carbide sanding discs to remove all scratches and blemishes.

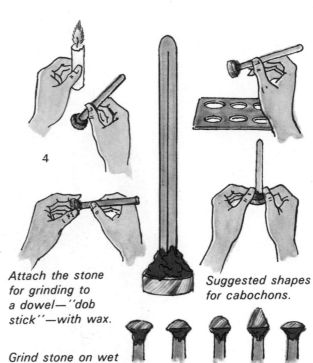

4

Attach the stone for grinding to a dowel—"dob stick"—with wax.

Suggested shapes for cabochons.

Grind stone on wet grindstone. Grind outline first, then grind the surface into shape desired.

5

Keep dob stick rocking and twirling.

6

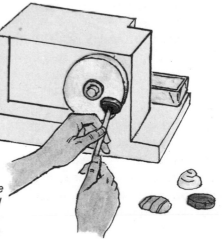

Final step is polishing, done with a small dab of polishing paste against a felt polishing wheel.

WEATHER

"Some are weather-wise, some are otherwise," Benjamin Franklin once said. In his day, it was very important for farmers and sailors to be "weather-wise"—to be able to figure out the weather for themselves by what knowledge they had picked up about weather signs. There was no one around, at that time, to give them a weather report every hour on the hour.

That's where we are lucky today. We get our daily weather reports, by radio or TV, based on the observations of thousands of people throughout the country—meteorologists, persons who specialize in weather.

But in addition to taking the experts' word for the weather, you will probably want to be able to do a bit of forecasting yourself. To do this, you need to have a general knowledge about what weather really is.

By dictionary definition, weather is "the state of the atmosphere with respect to heat or cold, wetness or dryness, calm or storm, clearness or cloudiness." Weather, in short, is the condition of the atmosphere. Without

atmosphere—that is, air—there is no weather.

Four different things go into making weather: heat, wind, moisture, and air pressure.

The heat, of course, comes from the sun, which heats up the earth, which in turn heats up the air above it. Heated air is lighter than cool air. It rises, and cool air rushes in in a cold wind to occupy its place. Knowing this fact you would think that a cold wind would be blowing steadily from the North Pole to take the place of the hot air rising over the equator. That would be the case except for the fact that the earth rotates around its axis. This rotation, from west to east, throws all major air movements off their direct courses. The result is that in our country most air currents —and, therefore, the weather in general— come from the West. The weather you have in your locality today is what people 500 miles to the west of you had yesterday if today is summer, 700 miles if today is winter.

The moisture in the air is what the air evaporates out of the oceans, lakes, and rivers over which it passes. The warmer the air, the more moisture it can contain. Most of this moisture is in the form of invisible vapor. If cooled, the moisture may form invisible clouds, or it may fall to the ground in liquid form as rain, or in solid form as snow.

These three features—heat, wind, moisture—provide the visible and "feelable" evidence of the weather. Together they influence the invisible air pressure which will vary in a given area according to coming weather. Before fair weather, the air is heavy, while before rainy weather, it becomes lighter.

With even this little bit of knowledge about what makes weather, you will be able to make your observations and arrive at your own deductions. You will then also find out that many of the old-time sayings of farmers and sailors—like those illustrated here—are true.

You will discover that *fair weather* is generally ahead when these are the weather signs:

The sun sets as a ball of fire or the sunset clouds are brilliantly red. (The sun sets in the west from which comes tomorrow's weather, and dry air, with its dust particles, produces a red glow.) Insect-eating birds, such as swallows, fly high. (Swallows catch and eat insects on the wing. At high air pressure, insects are carried up high by air currents.) The smoke from your campfire goes straight up in the air. (At high air pressure, smoke rises.) There is a heavy dew at night. (Dew forms when air moisture condenses on cooled-off vegetation during nights of dry air and clear skies.)

On the other hand, there's *poor weather* in store when you notice these signs:

The sunrise is red. (Dry weather is leaving toward the east, moist air is on the way from the west.) Swallows skim low over the lake. (At low air pressure, insects fly close to the ground on heavy, moist wings—the swallows follow.) Smoke curls downward. (Low air pressure prevents smoke from rising.) There is no dew at night. (On a cloudy night, vegetation does not cool off sufficiently for air moisture to condense on it.) The sky fills up with "scales" and "tails." ("Scales" and "tails" are cloud formations that warn of changing weather.) The moon has a ring around it. (Such a ring, or halo, forms when the moon shines through the ice crystals of cirrostratus clouds which precede poor weather.)

OLD WEATHER SAYINGS

Red sky at night, sailors' delight.
Red sky in morning, sailors take warning.

When heavy dew is on the grass,
Rain will never come to pass.

Swallows flying way up high
Tell there's no rain in the sky.

Mackerel scales and mares' tails
Make lofty ships carry low sails.

A ring around the moon means rain.
The larger the ring, the nearer the rain.

6 Miles
5 Miles
4 Miles
3 Miles
2 Miles
1 Mile

Cirrus

Cirrostratus

Thunderhead Cumulonimbus

Cirrocumulus

Altocumulus

Cumulonimbus

Altostratus

Stratocumulus

Cumulus

Nimbostratus

Stratus

Rain   Snow

Fog   Fog

CLOUDS

On a warm summer day, you may feel very uncomfortable—hot and sticky. And someone is sure to tell you, "It isn't the heat—it's the humidity." That statement will be right. The air around you is full of humidity, full of invisible water vapor. The warmer the air, the greater the amount.

Every day the heat of the sun evaporates millions of tons of water from oceans, lakes, and rivers up into the air. When the humidity-laden air gets cooled by ascending or expanding, some of the moisture condenses into droplets, and clouds form.

There are several ways of classifying clouds. They can be classified by altitude into four families: high clouds, middle clouds, low clouds, and towering clouds. Or we can simply classify them by their shapes into four general types: *cirrus*, featherlike; *stratus*, in a layer; *cumulus*, in heaps; *nimbus*, a scraggly cloud from which rain falls. These terms are often combined to make the description more exact. The word *alto*, high, may be put in front to indicate a cloud of high altitude.

Some clouds tell of fair weather. The altocumulus that drifts across the summer sky like a flock of white sheep is one of them. The cirrocumulus that looks somewhat like the scales of a fish—"mackerel sky"—sometimes brings windy, unsettled weather. Stratocumulus are grayish clouds, spread out in a rolling layer. The most beautiful clouds in the sky are the cumulus clouds. They resemble big puffs of cotton. But watch out for cumulus when it grows overly large and turns into cumulonimbus, "thunderhead." A violent storm will be upon you.

Poor weather, with rain—or snow in the winter—may be ahead when feathery whiffs of cirrus consolidate into cirrostratus, covering the face of the sun with a thin veil. This veil may soon start thickening into a complete overcast of altostratus. The rain will probably start falling within 10 to 15 hours as the steadily darkening clouds turn into nimbostratus. This is a sequence rarely broken except in hot weather, when the sun may evaporate the cirrus clouds.

Cloud Name	Abbrev.	What are the clouds made of?	What may fall from the clouds?	What weather do the clouds forecast?	How high?	What is the symbol?
Cirrus	Ci	Ice crystals	Nothing	Fair, but rain or snow if clouds thicken	4 miles or more	
Cirrostratus	Cs	Ice crystals	Nothing	Fair if they break up into cirrocumulus	4 miles or more	
Cirrocumulus	Cc	Ice crystals	Nothing	Rain if clouds thicken and lower	4 miles or more	
Altocumulus	Ac	Drops of water	Light rain or snow	Rain if corona around sun or moon decreases	1 to 4 miles	
Altostratus	As	Ice and water	Steady rain or snow	Storm if clouds darken toward the west	1 to 4 miles	
Stratocumulus	Sc	Drops of water	Drizzle or snow flurries	Changing weather	¼ to 1 mile	
Stratus	St	Drops of water	Drizzle or snow flurries	Fair weather, if clouds get smaller	0 to 1 mile	
Nimbostratus	Ns	Ice and water	Steady rain or snow	Long rainy stretch	0 to 1 mile	
Cumulus	Cu	Drops of water	Nothing	Generally fair	¼ to 4 miles	
Cumulonimbus	Cb	Ice and water	Heavy rain, snow or hail	Thunderstorms	¼ to 4 miles	

HOMEMADE BAROMETER

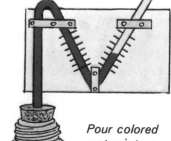

Pour colored water into a bent glass tube. Put tube in stopper in thermos bottle. Attach scale. Note level of water rising or falling.

THERMOMETER

Buy an inexpensive thermometer in a dime store. Hang in a shady place.

Read 3 times a day. Note especially sudden drops and rapid rises.

HYGROMETER

Remove fat from hair by soaking in carbon tetrachloride. Glue ends to top of board and to moving pointer.

Draw scale from radio weather reports.

WEATHER CLUE CHART						
LOOK FOR	WHEN					
	CLOUDS	HUMIDITY	PRESSURE	TEMP.	VISIBILITY	WINDS
Weather to stay FAIR	Move higher and decrease in numbers When morning fog disappears	Stays low	Remains steady or goes up slowly	Is what is expected for the season	Stays good	Are west to northwest and gentle
Weather to get WORSE	Thicken, lower and darken to the west	Goes up	Falls steadily or rapidly	Is too high or too low for season	Decreases	Shift to between east and south
RAIN or SNOW	Change from cirrus to lower types of rain or snow clouds	Goes up	Falls— the faster, the sooner rain or snow	Goes up	Decreases	Increase in speed, usually from the east
THUNDER-STORMS	Change from cumulus to cumulonimbus	— —	Falls	— —	— —	Increase in speed rapidly
Weather to CLEAR	Rise and break up	Goes down	Rises	Rises after warm front Drops after cold front	Increases	Swing from east through south to west
COLDER Weather	— —	— —	Rises	Goes down	— —	From north or northwest
WARMER Weather	— —	— —	Falls	Goes up	— —	From the south

RAIN GAUGE

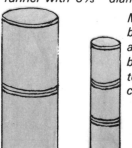

Cut circle with 5" radius from sheet tin.

Cut 120° from circle. Also cut 1"-radius center.

120°

Overlap and solder circle to make funnel with 6⅓" diameter opening.

Make 2 containers by soldering rims of 2 2-lb. coffee cans and 3 tomato paste cans, retaining bottom of bottom cans. Epoxy soup can to inside bottom of coffee can to support thin container. Set up gauge as shown above.

After a rain, measure water in thin container with yard stick. Divide by 10 to get rainfall.

WEATHER FORECASTING EQUIPMENT

Just as the Indians and farmers and sailors of old were able to judge the kind of weather ahead, you may be developing some of the same ability. But instead of depending completely on your judgement for determining changes in the weather, you may want to have the help of a few pieces of equipment in the forecasting:

Barometer for finding out the air pressure. When this goes up, fair weather is ahead. When it goes down, poor weather is approaching. It is not the exact reading of the barometer that counts, but whether it is falling or rising. A commercial barometer will show this quite definitely. So will a homemade barometer.

Thermometer to give you the temperature of the air. A commercial thermometer consists of a fine glass tube containing mercury. The mercury expands when it warms. This expansion is measured on a scale that shows you the number of degrees.

Hygrometer is used to tell the humidity in the air. There are several methods. One of them is using a long human hair, with the fat content removed, attached to a pointer. The hair picks up humidity—it lengthens when the humidity is high, shortens when it is low.

Weather vane gives you the direction of the wind. The wind scale below informs you of its speed.

WEATHER VANE

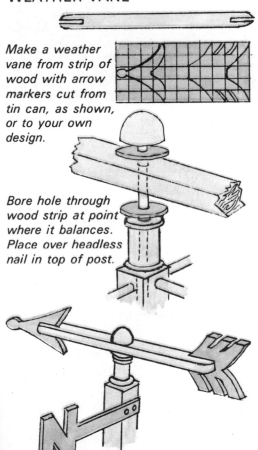

Make a weather vane from strip of wood with arrow markers cut from tin can, as shown, or to your own design.

Bore hole through wood strip at point where it balances. Place over headless nail in top of post.

Use washers to cut down friction, if needed, or suspend the vane by a tiny glass cup.

Mark the directions on the post either by an N (for North), cut from wood or sheet tin, or all main directions: N, W, S, E.

WIND CHART

Beaufort's Scale	How Fast? (Miles per hour)	What is it Called?	How Does it Show Itself?
0	0	No wind (calm)	Smoke moves up straight. Flag does not fly.
1	1 to 3	Slight wind	Wind pushes smoke slightly away from straight line.
2	4 to 7	Light breeze	Face feels wind. Leaves tremble.
3	8 to 12	Gentle breeze	Leaves flutter steadily. Flag begins to fly.
4	13 to 18	Moderate wind	Small branches move. Dust is lifted and blown about.
5	19 to 24	Fresh wind	Small trees with leaves begin to move.
6	25 to 31	Strong wind	Large branches move. Wires whistle.
7	32 to 38	High wind	Large trees begin to sway. The wind pushes you.
8	39 to 46	Gale	Small branches snap off trees. The wind begins to lift you.
9	47 to 54	Strong gale	Some damage to houses. Larger branches snap off trees.
10	55 to 63	Whole gale	Whole trees are snapped and uprooted.
11	64 to 75	Violent storm	Buildings are severely damaged, if unprotected.
12	75 and up	Hurricane	Almost everything movable or breakable in path destroyed.

SKY EXPLORING

For years and years and years and forever after, people around the world will worry about energy. ''Where are we going to get it? We're running out of oil, out of coal and natural gas.''

In the future, all energy—except for atomic power—will come from the same source from which energy has come since the creation of the world: from the sun, the center of our solar system. It's the sun that makes possible life on earth today. And it was the sun, ages ago, that gave life to the prehistoric plants that turned into coal and gas; to the ancient plant and animal matter that became oil. By the time we have used up all our mineral fuels, our inventors will have learned to turn the sun's heat into ever-available energy.

The moon may also help. The tides are

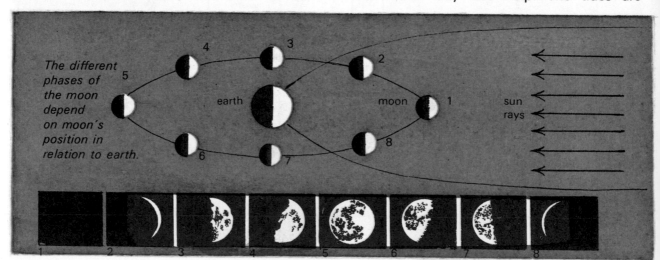

The different phases of the moon depend on moon's position in relation to earth.

earth

moon

sun rays

Polestar, Cassiopeia, and Big Dipper at 8:00 PM on January 15, March 15, June 15, October 15.

caused by the gravity of the moon. As the earth turns, the oceans of the world send tides up against the landmasses. So far, we have not made effective use of this energy. The time will come when we will.

The sun is a star—that is, a heavenly body that gives out light and heat of its own. The moon is a satellite—a dead mineral mass with no light of its own. Moonshine is only reflected sunshine. The sun always lights up half of the moon, but because of the different positions of earth and moon as they travel around the sun, we only see the moon fully illuminated at full-moon time. At other times it appears as a crescent or a half-moon.

Although our sun is immense as compared to the earth, it is only a minor star among the billions of stars of the universe. Some of these stars seem to form patterns in the night sky. We call them constellations.

If the earth turned around its axis in exactly 24 hours, we would always see the same constellations in the sky. But it doesn't. The earth makes its turn in only about 23 hours and 56 minutes. The result is that the constellations rise nearly 4 minutes earlier on each successive night—2 hours a month, 6 hours a season, 24 hours a year. So, if you watch the sky at the same time of the night, once a week, once a month, even once a season, in a year's time you will see all the stars visible in your location. If you made it 8:00 PM on January 15, March 15, June 15, and October 15, you would be able to follow the Big Dipper and Cassiopeia and all the stars of the Northern sky making their complete swings around the polestar or across the sky.

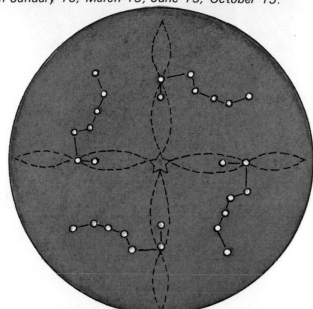

The ancient symbol known as the ''swastika'' may have represented the seasonal positions of the Big Dipper.

horizon line

Paint the constellations on inside of an umbrella and use to show movement of the stars.

101

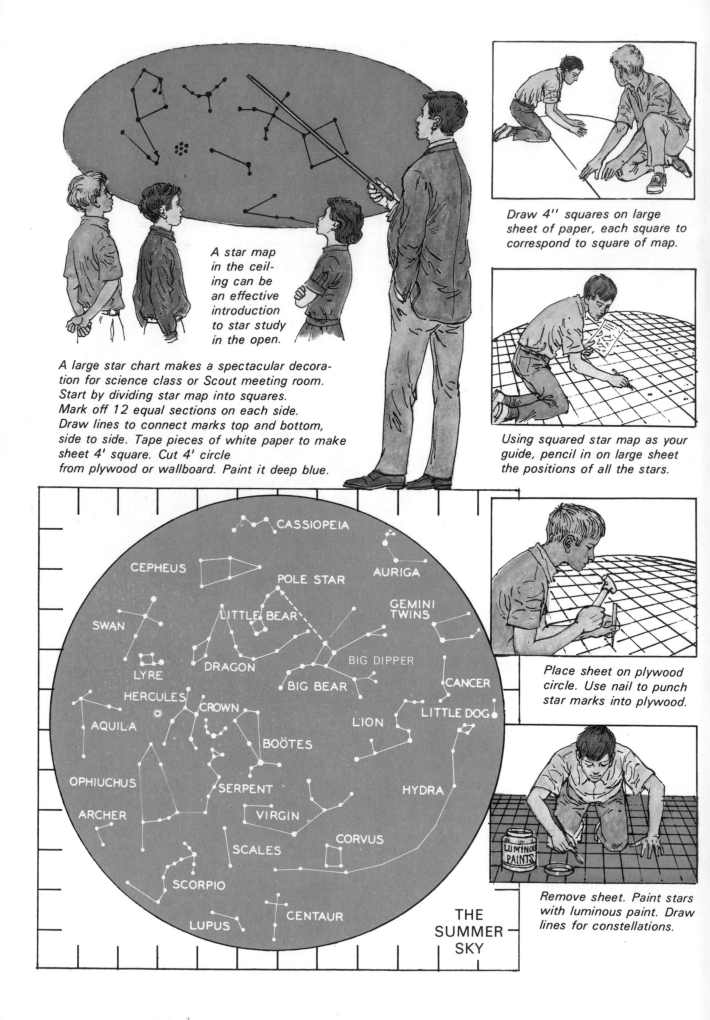

A star map in the ceiling can be an effective introduction to star study in the open.

A large star chart makes a spectacular decoration for science class or Scout meeting room. Start by dividing star map into squares. Mark off 12 equal sections on each side. Draw lines to connect marks top and bottom, side to side. Tape pieces of white paper to make sheet 4' square. Cut 4' circle from plywood or wallboard. Paint it deep blue.

Draw 4'' squares on large sheet of paper, each square to correspond to square of map.

Using squared star map as your guide, pencil in on large sheet the positions of all the stars.

Place sheet on plywood circle. Use nail to punch star marks into plywood.

Remove sheet. Paint stars with luminous paint. Draw lines for constellations.

THE SUMMER SKY

CASSIOPEIA
CEPHEUS
AURIGA
POLE STAR
LITTLE BEAR
GEMINI TWINS
SWAN
DRAGON
BIG DIPPER
LYRE
BIG BEAR
CANCER
HERCULES
CROWN
LITTLE DOG
AQUILA
LION
BOÖTES
OPHIUCHUS
SERPENT
HYDRA
ARCHER
VIRGIN
CORVUS
SCALES
SCORPIO
CENTAUR
LUPUS

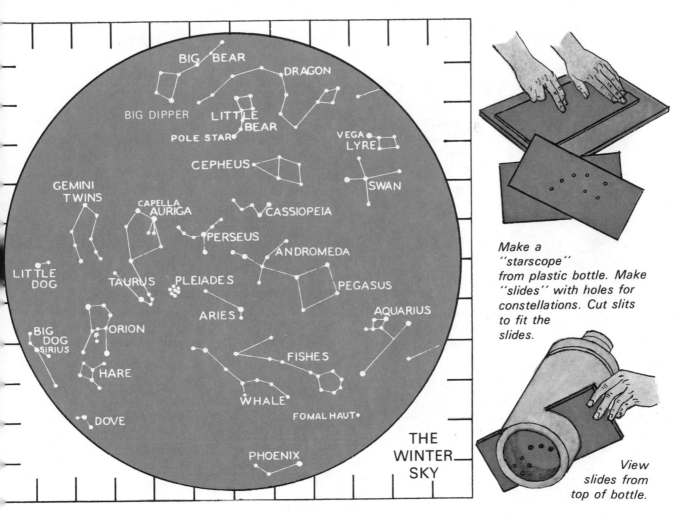

BIG BEAR

DRAGON

BIG DIPPER

LITTLE BEAR

POLE STAR

VEGA
LYRE

CEPHEUS

SWAN

GEMINI
TWINS

CAPELLA
AURIGA

CASSIOPEIA

PERSEUS

ANDROMEDA

LITTLE
DOG

TAURUS

PLEIADES

PEGASUS

ARIES

AQUARIUS

BIG
DOG
SIRIUS

ORION

FISHES

HARE

WHALE

FOMALHAUT

DOVE

THE
WINTER
SKY

PHOENIX

Make a
"starscope"
from plastic bottle. Make
"slides" with holes for
constellations. Cut slits
to fit the
slides.

View
slides from
top of bottle.

STUDYING THE STARS

If this is summer, look at the star map showing the summer sky. If this is winter, study the map of the winter sky. In either case, begin your star study by locating the Big Bear, then finding in this constellation the part we call the Big Dipper: the four stars that make up the bowl and the three stars that make up the handle—or, rather, the four, because one of the three is a double star. Now draw an imaginary line between the two stars of the bowl farthest from the handle and continue this line until you hit the polestar—the North Star. Next, locate, on the opposite side of the polestar, the W-shaped Cassiopeia.

With the positions of the Big Dipper and Cassiopeia in relation to the polestar clearly in your mind, you can now set out to find other major constellations: on the summer map, kite-shaped Boötes, crescent-shaped Crown, H-shaped Hercules, cross-shaped Swan, sickle-shaped Lion, the two bright stars of the

Twins. On the winter map you should be able to locate house-shaped Cepheus, man-shaped Orion, square-shaped Pegasus, the V-shaped head of Taurus (the Bull), the Pleiades.

After a bit of map study, you are ready to go out into the night to locate the constellations in the sky. Hold the respective star map overhead, turn it until you have the Big Dipper, the polestar, and Cassiopeia lined up. Then go on from there.

If you are particularly thorough in your study of the sky, you may one night discover a couple of stars not indicated on the map. They would not be real stars, shining by their own light, but planets, shining by light reflected from the sun. Depending on the time of year and the time of night, you might be seeing Venus or Jupiter, Saturn or Mars. To learn which they are, get hold of an almanac and check up on what planets are supposed to be in the sky at the time you are watching.

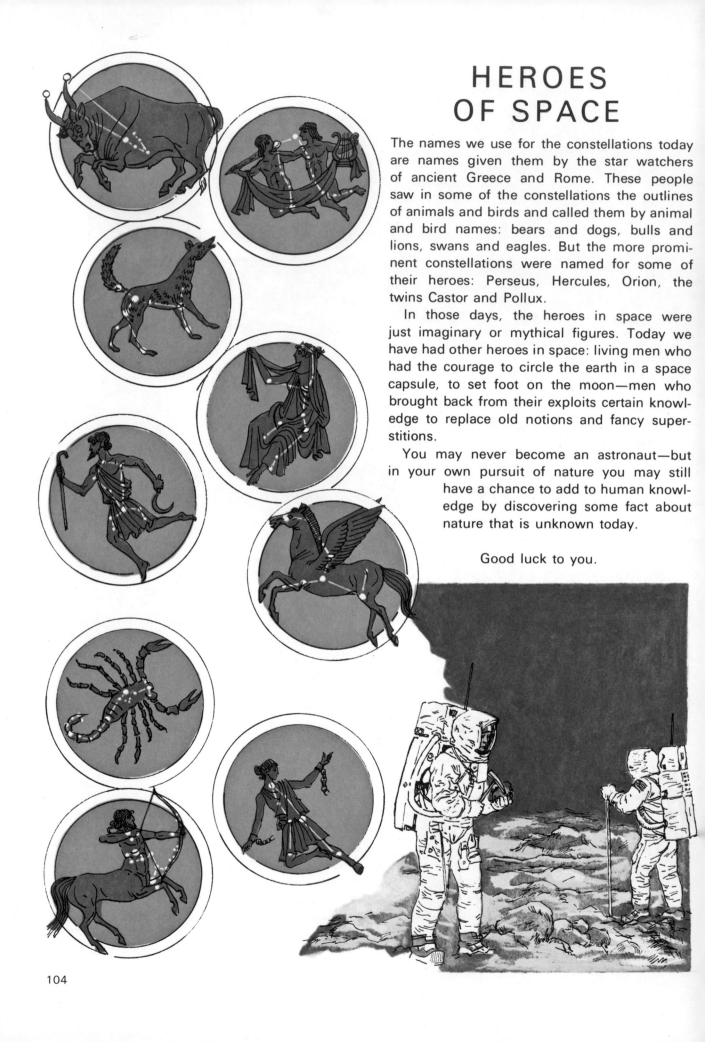

HEROES OF SPACE

The names we use for the constellations today are names given them by the star watchers of ancient Greece and Rome. These people saw in some of the constellations the outlines of animals and birds and called them by animal and bird names: bears and dogs, bulls and lions, swans and eagles. But the more prominent constellations were named for some of their heroes: Perseus, Hercules, Orion, the twins Castor and Pollux.

In those days, the heroes in space were just imaginary or mythical figures. Today we have had other heroes in space: living men who had the courage to circle the earth in a space capsule, to set foot on the moon—men who brought back from their exploits certain knowledge to replace old notions and fancy superstitions.

You may never become an astronaut—but in your own pursuit of nature you may still have a chance to add to human knowledge by discovering some fact about nature that is unknown today.

Good luck to you.

BOOKS TO READ AND USE

BOOKS FOR READING

Your local library will have a great number of books that will introduce you to all phases of nature. You may want to start by looking up some of the following:

NEW GOLDEN TREASURY OF NATURAL HISTORY by Bertha Morris Parker

THE SEA AROUND US by Rachel Carson

LIFE Nature Library: THE BIRDS, THE MAMMALS, THE REPTILES, THE INSECTS, THE FISHES, THE PLANTS, THE EARTH, THE UNIVERSE, ECOLOGY

ECOLOGY by Tayler R. Alexander and George S. Fichter

EASY GUIDES FOR IDENTIFICATION

The *Golden Nature Guide* series is excellent for simple identification. All the books listed below were developed under the editorship of Herbert S. Zim. Most of them were co-authored by Zim and the expert named after the titles below:

BIRDS Ira N. Gabrielsen

MAMMALS Donald F. Hoffmeister

REPTILES AND AMPHIBIANS Hobart Smith

FISHES Hurst H. Shoemaker

POND LIFE George K. Reid

SEASHORES Lester Ingle

SEASHELLS OF THE WORLD R. Tucker Abbott

INSECTS Clarence Cottam

BUTTERFLIES AND MOTHS Robert T. Mitchell

FLOWERS Alexander C. Martin

NON-FLOWERING PLANTS Floyd S. Shuttleworth

TREES Alexander C. Martin

ROCKS AND MINERALS Paul R. Shaffer

FOSSILS Frank H. T. Rhodes and Paul R. Shaffer

WEATHER Paul E. Lahr and R. Will Burnett

STARS Robert H. Baker

ADVANCED BOOKS FOR IDENTIFICATION

As in the case of books for reading, the best trick, before you decide to buy an advanced book on identification, is for you to look it up in your local library.

BIRDS

BIRDS OF NORTH AMERICA by Chandler S. Robbins, Bertel Bruun, and Herbert S. Zim

FIELD GUIDE TO THE BIRDS and FIELD GUIDE TO WESTERN BIRDS by Roger Tory Peterson

FIELD BOOK OF EASTERN BIRDS by Leon A. Hausman

AUDUBON LAND BIRD GUIDE and AUDUBON WATER BIRD GUIDE by Richard H. Pough

MAMMALS

FIELD BOOK OF NORTH AMERICAN MAMMALS by H. E. Anthony

FIELD GUIDE TO THE MAMMALS by W. H. Burt and R. P. Grossenheider

MAMMAL GUIDE: MAMMALS OF NORTH AMERICA by Ralph S. Palmer

REPTILES AND AMPHIBIANS

NEW FIELD BOOK OF REPTILES AND AMPHIBIANS by Doris M. Cochran and Coleman J. Goin

FIELD GUIDE TO REPTILES AND AMPHIBIANS by Roger Conant

INSECTS

FIELD BOOK OF INSECTS by Frank K. Lutz

FIELD GUIDE TO THE INSECTS OF AMERICA NORTH OF MEXICO by Donald J. Borror and Richard E. White

FIELD GUIDE TO THE BUTTERFLIES by Alexander B. Klots

WATER LIFE
Freshwater Life

NEW FIELD BOOK OF FRESHWATER LIFE by Elsie B. Klots

Saltwater Life

FIELD BOOK OF SEASHORE LIFE by Roy Waldo Miner

FIELD BOOK OF MARINE FISHES OF THE ATLANTIC COAST by Charles M. Breder

Shells

SEASHELLS OF NORTH AMERICA by R. Tucker Abbott

FIELD GUIDE TO THE SHELLS OF OUR ATLANTIC AND GULF COASTS and

FIELD GUIDE TO THE SHELLS OF THE PACIFIC COAST AND HAWAII by Percy A. Morris

FLOWERS

FIELD GUIDE TO WILDFLOWERS OF NORTHEASTERN AND NORTH-CENTRAL NORTH AMERICA by Roger Tory Peterson and Margaret McKenny

NEW FIELD BOOK OF AMERICAN WILD FLOWERS by Harold W. Rickett

WILD FLOWER GUIDE by Edgar T. Wherry

TREES

TREES OF NORTH AMERICA by C. Frank Brockman

FIELD GUIDE TO TREES AND SHRUBS by George A. Petrides

ROCKS AND MINERALS

FIELD GUIDE TO ROCKS AND MINERALS by F. H. Pough

FIELD BOOK OF COMMON ROCKS AND MINERALS by Frederic B. Loomis

STARS

FIELD GUIDE TO THE STARS AND PLANETS by Donald H. Menzel

THE SKY OBSERVER'S GUIDE by R. Newton Mayall, Margaret Mayall, and Jerome Wyckoff

MORE OUTDOOR THINGS TO DO

After you have done some of the things suggested in this Golden Book of *Outdoor Things to Do*, you may want to continue with many more projects in your field of interest. You will find hundreds of more ideas in the book that has become the standard handbook for nature-interested individuals, nature clubs and camps, Scout troops and patrols:

NEW FIELD BOOK OF NATURE ACTIVITIES AND HOBBIES by William Hillcourt

INDEX

Numbers in bold type refer to pictures and captions